PENGU
SPEAKIN

Satyajit Ray (1921–92) was one of the greatest film-makers of his time. Starting with *Pather Panchali*, which won an award at the Cannes Film Festival and established Ray as a director of international stature, Ray made such all-time classics as *Aparajito*, *Apur Sansar*, *Charulata*, *Ashani Sanket*, *Kanchanjungha*, *Aranyer Din Ratri*, *Ghare Baire* and *Agantuk*. He also made several documentaries, including one on Tagore and another on his father Sukumar Ray, Bengal's most famous writer of nonsense verse and children's books. Both the British Federation of Film Societies and the Moscow Film Festival Committee named Ray one of the greatest directors of the second half of the twentieth century. In 1992, he was awarded the Oscar for Lifetime Achievement by the Academy of Motion Picture Arts and Sciences and, in the same year, was also honoured with the Bharat Ratna.

Ray was also a writer of repute, and his short stories, novellas, poems and articles, written in Bengali, have been immensely popular ever since they first began to appear in the children's magazine *Sandesh* in 1961. He has published several books in Bengali, most of which became best-sellers. He is also the author of *Our Films, Their Films* and *Bishay Chalachitra*, both immensely popular books of essays on cinema.

Gopa Majumdar has translated several works from Bengali to English, the most notable of these being Ashapurna Debi's *Subarnalata* and Bibhuti Bhushan Bandopadhyay's *Aparajito*, for which she won the Sahitya Akademi Award in 2001. She has translated several volumes of Satyajit Ray's short stories and all of the Feluda stories for Penguin Books India.

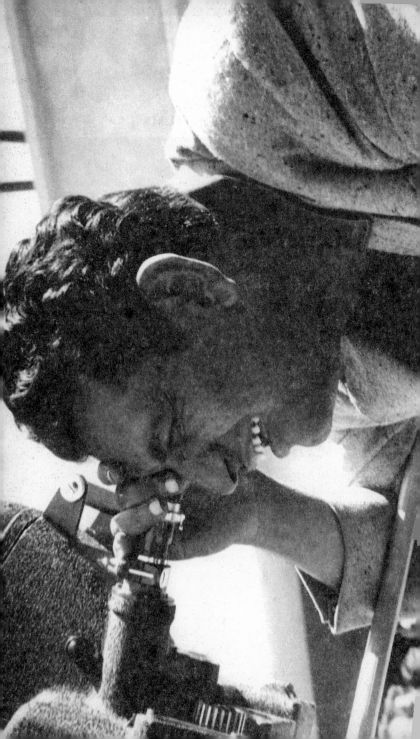

Speaking of Films

SATYAJIT RAY

Translated from the Bengali
by
Gopa Majumdar

PENGUIN BOOKS

PENGUIN BOOKS
Published by the Penguin Group
Penguin Books India Pvt. Ltd, 11 Community Centre, Panchsheel Park, New
Delhi 110 017, India
Penguin Group (USA) Inc., 375 Hudson Street, New York, New York 10014,
USA
Penguin Group (Canada), 90 Eglinton Avenue East, Suite 700, Toronto,
Ontario, M4P 2Y3, Canada (a division of Pearson Penguin Canada Inc.)
Penguin Books Ltd, 80 Strand, London WC2R 0RL, England
Penguin Ireland, 25 St Stephen's Green, Dublin 2, Ireland (a division of Penguin
Books Ltd)
Penguin Group (Australia), 250 Camberwell Road, Camberwell, Victoria
3124, Australia (a division of Pearson Australia Group Pty Ltd)
Penguin Group (NZ), 67 Apollo Drive, Rosedale, North Shore 0632, New
Zealand (a division of Pearson New Zealand Ltd)
Penguin Group (South Africa) (Pty) Ltd, 24 Sturdee Avenue, Rosebank,
Johannesburg 2196, South Africa

Penguin Books Ltd, Registered Offices: 80 Strand, London WC2R 0RL,
England

Originally published in Bengali as *Bishay Chalachitra*, by Ananda Publishers
Private Limited, 1982
First published in English by Penguin Books India 2005

Typeset by Eleven Arts, Keshav Puram, New Delhi
Printed at Pauls Press, New Delhi

Contents

Foreword

Fans of Satyajit Ray's cinema will certainly be familiar with *Our Films, Their Films*, a collection of his writings on cinema that was published in 1976. Readers and moviegoers outside of Bengal may not have heard, however, of *Bishay Chalachitra*, a compilation of Ray's articles on cinema written in Bengali. These articles were written over a span of twenty-five years and address issues not covered in *Our Films, Their Films*. The first article in *Bishay Chalachitra* dates back to 1955, the year that *Pather Panchali*, Ray's first film, was released. The remaining pieces in the book deal with various aspects of Indian and international cinema and contain extremely interesting comments from Ray on his own art.

This is the very first time that *Bishay Chalachitra* is appearing in translation—and thus, for the first time, readers outside Bengal will be able to read these 'lost' pieces on cinema by the master film-maker. I must commend Gopa Majumdar for her marvellous translation that brings Ray's writings to life in English. *Speaking of Films* also contains 'My Life, My Work', the text of the Amal Bhattacharji lecture that Satyajit Ray delivered in 1982, which is being published in book form for the very first time.

Speaking of Films is being published on the fiftieth anniversary of the release of *Pather Panchali*—a fitting occasion for Ray's writings on cinema to reach out to newer audiences than ever before. I hope this book finds the widest readership across India as well as abroad.

Kolkata
2 May 2005   Sandip Ray

My Life, My Work

When I was asked to deliver their annual lecture by the Amal Bhattacharji Centre for European Studies, my immediate response was to say no. It was easy for me to do so, since fifteen years of saying no to such requests has turned it into a habit. On the only occasion I didn't decline, the lecture never took place.

Although I had, in the end, to yield to persuasion, a great deal of diffidence remains. It is difficult to dissociate the idea of discourse from the idea of erudition; especially in the present case, where the enterprise is meant to perpetuate the memory of an outstanding scholar. Now, erudition is something I singularly lack. As a student, I was only a little better than average, and, in all honesty, I cannot say that what I learnt in school and college has stood me in good stead in the years that followed. I studied for a degree, of course, but my best and keenest memories of college consist largely of the quirks and idiosyncrasies of certain professors. College was fun, but college, at least for me, was hardly a fount of learning. All my useful reading has taken place after I finished my formal education. This reading has been wide and varied, but it has

---

From the Amal Bhattacharji Memorial Lecture 1982.

not been deep. Even on films, I am not particularly well read. When I got interested enough in films to start reading about them, there were hardly a dozen books in English on the subject. By the time I finished them, I was already at work on my first film. One day's work with camera and actors taught me more than all the dozen books had done. In other words, I learnt about film-making primarily by making films, not by reading books on the art of the cinema. Here, I must say, I am in very good company. This is how all the pioneers of film-making learnt their craft. But for a few exceptions, none of these pioneers was a learned scholar. Rather, they liked to think of themselves as craftsmen. If they were also able, on occasion, to produce works of art, they often did so intuitively. Or at least, that is how most of them feel. The famous American director John Ford was once asked by an admiring critic how he got the idea for a particularly felicitous touch in one of his films. Ford said: 'Aw, I don't know, it just came to me.'

This brings me to the second reason for my diffidence. Film-making is such a demanding process that directors— especially those who keep up a steady output—rarely have time to assemble their thoughts. Of all the major directors in the world, only one—Sergei Eisenstein—lectured and theorized on cinema, and described his own creative process at length. But we must remember that in the space of nearly twenty years, Eisenstein made only seven films, of which two were never completed. I have regularly pursued my two vocations of film-making and writing for young people, untrammelled by any thoughts of ever having to describe or analyse why I do certain things in the way I do them.

Yet a third reason concerns a special problem that faces one who must talk about films. Lectures on art should ideally be illustrated. One who talks on paintings usually comes armed with slides and a projector. This solves the difficulty of having to describe in words, what must be seen with the eyes. The lecturer on music must bless the silicon revolution, which enables him to cram all his examples onto a cassette no bigger than a small bar of chocolate. But the lecturer on cinema has no such advantage—at least not in the present state of technology in our country. If he wishes to cite an example, he can do no more than give a barely adequate description in words, of what is usually perceived with all one's senses. A film is pictures, a film is words, a film is movement, a film is drama, a film is music, a film is a story, a film is a thousand expressive aural and visual details. These days one must also add that film is colour. Even a segment of film that lasts barely a minute can display all these aspects simultaneously. You will realize what a hopeless task it is to describe a scene from a film in words. They can't even begin to do justice to a language which is so complex.

So when it was suggested that I talk on European cinema, I declined. I didn't wish to talk about films which would be unfamiliar to many of the listeners. Even reading about such films can be tiresome. But at least, with a book, one can stop reading, and think, and try to visualize. Unfortunately, it is not easy to stop a lecturer, and ask for time to think. At least, it is not *conventional* to do so.

So I shall avoid describing films which the majority of my listeners are unlikely to have seen. I should also make it clear that I do not propose to discuss cinema in all its aspects. You will not learn about its history from this talk, nor about its sociology, its economics, its semiology. Nor will you learn about the New Wave, the star system, or the regional cinema, and what the governments are doing to help or hinder its growth. I shall confine myself mainly to the language of films, and the possibilities of artistic expression inherent in it. This will involve an occasional glance at the other arts, as well as at films from other countries and other epochs. My main concern, however, will be Bengal, the Bengali cinema, and my own films.

But before I get to the subject of films, I should like to recall the gradual stages which led to my being involved in this very versatile, very popular and very chancy medium. One thing I cannot avoid in this talk is the first person singular. This is a fact which had better be conveyed now, lest the listeners spot it on their own and begin to question my modesty. There is no one I know better than myself, and no one I have a better right to talk about.

On the strength of my first film and the wide success it won, I have heard it said that I was a born film-maker. And yet, I had no thoughts, and no ambitions, of ever becoming one even as late as three or four years before I actually took the plunge. I loved going to the cinema ever since I can remember, but I must have shared this love with millions of others, or there wouldn't be such a flourishing film business in India for such a long time.

I was born in the heyday of silent cinema. Chaplin, Keaton and Harold Lloyd were producing what *then* were uproarious comedies, and are *now* seen as timeless masterpieces. Living in North Calcutta then, and most of the cinemas showing foreign films being around Chowringhee, going to the 'Bioscope' was a rare event. So I never had a surfeit of films. Every visit was a very special occasion, and every film was followed by weeks of musing on its wonders.

When the talkies came, I was just old enough to realize that a revolution had taken place. There were two kinds of talkies to start with: Partial Talkies, which had bursts of dialogue, followed by long stretches of silence; and One Hundred Per

Cent Talkies. Newspapers in those days carried large pictorial ads of the foreign films. One look at them and a glance at the headlines were enough to tell the elders whether or not the films were likely to tarnish innocent minds. Those were the days of the flamboyant Hollywood stars, and what they were good at was not considered particularly suitable for a boy barely in his teens. So 'sizzling romance' was out, and so was 'tempestuous, hot-blooded passion'. I saw jungle stories, slapstick comedies, and swashbuckling adventures. But occasionally there were chance visits to supposedly adult movies. Ernst Lubitsch was a great name in cinema those days. As an Austrian who had settled in Hollywood, he had a highly sophisticated approach to romantic comedy. I saw three of his films, around the age of ten: *Love Parade*, *The Smiling Lieutenant* and *One Hour With You*—a forbidden world, only half understood, but observed with a tingling curiosity.

Films remained a great attraction right through college. But by then I had discovered something which was to grow into an obsession. This was western classical music. I had grown up in an atmosphere of Bengali songs, mainly Rabindrasangeet and Brahmo Samaj hymns. Even as a child, the ones that I liked most had a western tinge to them. A Vedic hymn like *Sangachhadhwam*, or the song by Rabindranath with a rather similar tune, *Anandalokay mangalalokay*; or the stately chorus, *Padoprantay rakho shebokey*, which came as a wonderful relief after three exhausting hours of sermon on Maghotsab day. My response to western classical music was immediate and decisive. As a small boy, I had read about Beethoven in the *Book of Knowledge*, and developed an admiration for him which amounted to hero-worship. Now I was listening enraptured to his sonatas and symphonies. If films were fun and thrills and escape, the pursuit of music was something undertaken with deadly seriousness. It was a great voyage of discovery, and it transported me to a world of ineffable delight. Films were at the most a once-a-week affair, while music, played on the hand-cranked gramophone, took up all my spare time at home. At an age when the Bengali youth almost inevitably writes poetry, I was listening to European classical music.

My reading was then confined to light English fiction. I hardly read any Bengali those days; not even the classics. In fact, I was not conscious of any roots in Bengal at all. That happened in Santiniketan.

THE WORLD OF SANTINIKETAN

The few occasions that I met Rabindranath face to face—well, meeting is hardly the word: one stole up to him with one's heart in one's mouth, and touched his feet—he would glance up at my mother and say: 'Why don't you send your son to my school?'

To be quite honest, I had no wish to go to his school at all. The few Santiniketanites that I got to know—usually painters and musicians—all had long hair, and spoke Bengali in a strange affected sing-song. One took this to be the Santiniketan accent. Well, such accent and such people put me off, and I thought—if this is what Santiniketan did to you, I had no use for that place.

When, after my graduation, I did go to Santiniketan, it was out of deference to my mother's wish, and much against my own inclination. I think my mother believed that proximity to Rabindranath would have a therapeutic effect on me, much as a visit to a hill station or health resort has on one's system.

Although I joined as a student of Kalabhawan, I had no wish to become a painter—certainly not a painter of the Oriental school. I strongly disliked the wishy-washy sentimentalism of Oriental art one encountered in the pages of *Probashi* and *Modern Review*. I had shown a flair for drawing from a very early age, doubtless inherited, and my taste in painting had been formed by the same ten-volume *Book of Knowledge* which had told me about Beethoven.

The *Book of Knowledge* left out everything before the Renaissance, and ended with the Royal Academicians. Among the paintings and sculptures I knew and loved were: Gainsborough's *Blue Boy*, Franz Hals's *Laughing Cavalier*, Michelangelo's *David*, Rodin's *Thinker*, Landseer's proud stag with the spreading antlers, and Joshua Reynold's *Bubbles*, which, in those days, was used in advertisements for Pear's Soap. Of course, I also knew Raphael's *Madonna*, and Da Vinci's *Mona Lisa*. I read somewhere that Mona Lisa's right hand was the most beautifully executed hand in all painting. I would gaze at this hand, and marvel at the critic who had studied all the paintings of the world, and come to that conclusion.

Since I never meant to complete the five-year course of Kalabhawan, I left at the end of two-and-a-half. Rabindranath had died a year before. It was hard for me to judge if it had made a material difference to the place; after all, he had been virtually invisible to us much of the time. But with everybody saying 'it's not the same thing any more' one found oneself concurring. But the main reason I left was not because Rabindranath was no more, but because I felt I had got as much out of the place as was possible for me.

My relationship with Santiniketan was an ambivalent one. As one born and bred in Calcutta, I loved to mingle with the crowd on Chowringhee, to hunt for bargains in the teeming profusion of second-hand books on the pavements of College Street, to explore the grimy depths of Chor Bazaar for symphonies at throwaway prices, to relax in the coolness of a cinema, and lose myself in the make-believe world of

Hollywood. All this I missed in Santiniketan, which was a world apart. It was a world of vast open spaces, vaulted over with a dustless sky that on a clear night showed the constellations as no city sky could ever do. The same sky, on a clear day, could summon up in moments an awesome invasion of billowing darkness that seemed to engulf the entire universe. And there was the *khoaai*, rimmed with serried ranks of taal trees, and the *Kopai*, snaking its way through its rough-hewn undulations. If Santiniketan did nothing else, it induced contemplation, and a sense of wonder, in the most prosaic and earthbound of minds.

In the two-and-a-half years, I had time to think, and time to realize that, almost without my being aware of it, the place had opened windows for me. More than anything else, it had brought to me an awareness of our tradition, which I knew would serve as a foundation for any branch of art that I wished to pursue.

But my attitude to painting as a vocation did not change. The first painting I did as a student showed a very old, blind beggar standing in the middle of nowhere, leaning on the shoulder of an angelic-looking boy who carried the begging bowl. My later paintings improved, as I moved away from literary themes, but I just didn't have it in me to become a painter.

But Santiniketan taught me two things—to look at paintings, and to look at nature. We used to go out in the afternoon to sketch from nature. Nandalal Bose, our Mastermoshai, would steal up from behind, peer over the shoulder and say: 'That's a good outline of a cow. But a cow is more than an outline. You must feel the form of the animal— the flesh and bones beneath the skin, and this feeling must show in the way your pencil moves.'

It was Santiniketan which opened my eyes to the fact that

the kind of painting I used to admire, the kind that provokes the reaction, 'How lifelike', should be a preoccupation that lasted only 400 years. It started with the first awareness of perspective in the fifteenth century, and ended with the invention of photography in the nineteenth. The first representations of nature by man are believed to be the stone-age cave paintings of 20,000 years ago. What is 400 years in a span that stretches 200 centuries?

Neither Egyptian, nor Chinese, Japanese or Indian art ever concerned itself with factual representation. Here, the primary aim was to get at the essence of things; a probing beneath the surface. Nature was the point of departure for the artist to arrive at a personal vision. Personal, but within the ambit of certain well-defined conventions.

Two trips to the great art centres of India—Ajanta, Ellora, Elephanta, Konarak and others—consolidated the idea of Indian tradition in my mind. At last I was beginning to find myself, and find my roots.

What I missed most in Santiniketan was films. Almost imperceptibly, they had become an object of study, as music was, and not something to be just seen and enjoyed. I had found and read a couple of books on film aesthetics in the Kalabhawan library. They were most revealing. How interesting to know, for instance, that films and music had so much in common! Both unfold over a period of time; both are concerned with pace and rhythm and contrast; both can be described in terms of mood—sad, cheerful, pensive, boisterous, tragic, jubilant. But this resemblance applies only to western classical music. Since our music is improvised, its pattern and duration are flexible. One can hear a complete raga in a three-minute version on old gramophone records, and we know that a raga can be stretched to well over two hours. Also, the structure of Indian music is decorative, not dramatic. It builds up from a slow beginning to a fast conclusion, becoming more and more intricate and ornamental in the process. This is rather like an Indian temple, which builds up from a solid base, goes through narrower and narrower layers of ornamentation, and ends up in the dizzy heights of the *shikhara*. The mood of the music is predetermined by the raga, and convention demands that there should be no departure from it. What the musician aims at is to give the ideal form to the concept implicit in a particular combination of notes. That is why Indian music is great only in the hands of a great musician performing at the top of his form. In the process of execution, the musician can achieve beauty, he can achieve tension and excitement, and he can achieve sublimity. But he cannot achieve drama, because there is no conflict in the music.

Unlike Indian music, Western music can depart from the tonic or Sa, and much of the drama arises from this modulation of certain basic melodies from key to key. This can be likened to the vicissitudes experienced by characters in a story. At the end, the music has to return to the tonic or Sa, which again is like the resolution of a conflict, where one feels that nothing more needs to be said, as the drama has come to an end.

It is significant that most of the pioneers of cinema—those who helped to create its grammar and its language—Griffith in USA, Abel Gance in France, Eisenstein and Pudovkin in Soviet Russia—were all deeply responsive to music. Griffith virtually created the language of cinema single-handed. It took him a little while to realize the incredible potentialities of the medium, but once he saw that images could be invested with meaning, and such meaningful images could be strung together like sentences in story, and the story could be made to unfold with the grace and fluency of music, the art of cinema evolved in no time at all.

In the early days, when books on film aesthetics had yet to be written, film-makers who were in the forefront were geniuses who instinctively produced works of art which at the same time had a wide appeal. That films had to reach a large public was taken for granted, since film-making was a costly business. But the wonder is how little pandering this involved. The one obvious concession to the public was in the use of slapstick, which was a direct importation from the music hall and vaudeville. But in the hands of a film-maker of genius, even slapstick could be so inventive, so precise in timing and so elaborate in execution that it acquired a high aesthetic value, while retaining its power to provoke laughter. Buster Keaton in his film *The General* performs the most incredible antics in the driver's seat of a runaway train, while a full-scale battle rages in the background. To say that the scene is funny is not nearly enough; it is one of the most elating aesthetic experiences in cinema.

Unfortunately, this double function of artist and entertainer was rarely sustained in the period of sound. Popular entertainment, too often, came to mean films of overt escapism, where the artist was conspicuous by his absence.

ONLY A *RASIKA* CAN APPRECIATE A WORK OF ART

It is not easy to define what gives a film the distinction of a work of art. Some definitions will emerge in course of this talk, but it is necessary at this point to stress the fact that to be able to tell a work of art from a work of mere craftsmanship calls for a trained response. In other words, it calls for what the shastras define as a rasika. One wouldn't think so from the way seemingly learned opinions on this or that film are bandied about by all and sundry. Nevertheless, it is true that serious, accomplished films—films which use the language of cinema with insight and imagination—challenge our sensibilities in the same way as the more rarefied forms of music, painting and literature. Even an apparently simple film which makes a direct impact on the emotions may call for understanding.

It was my growing interest in cinema as an object for serious study which led to our forming the Calcutta Film Society in the year of India's independence. Most of the films we showed and discussed were from abroad. To be quite honest, we found nothing worth studying in Bengali films from an aesthetic point of view. But it was interesting to try and discover why they were like what they were.

There is little doubt that the Bengali's fondness for the theatre and jatra was one of the things which impeded the growth of a pure cinema in Bengal. When one watched the shooting of a film in the studio, as I had done on several occasions, one had the strong feeling of watching the performance of a play. Rooms had three walls and no ceilings, windows gave on crudely painted backdrops, dummy books lined the shelves, and the performers appeared plastered with make-up. Right from the start, speech was taken as the primary means of conveying information, with images and gestures hardly given a chance to speak for themselves. Songs and melodrama, standard prescription for Bengali films, were direct imports from the stage. Such was the Bengali's fondness for songs that K.L. Saigal became a popular hero, and no questions asked either about his Bengali accent, which was redolent of the Punjab, or his acting ability, which was rudimentary.

The fact that some of the leading Bengali writers of the

time—Sailajananda Mukherji, Premankur Atarthi, Premendra Mitra, Saradindu Bandopadhyay—were involved in films as writers or directors or both, did little to improve the quality of Bengali films. When writing fiction or poetry, these writers obviously aimed at a literate public; but when writing for films or directing them, they seemed to assume a totally different identity, and aim at the lowest of lowbrows. Occasionally, one would come across a believable character, or a situation with a breath of life in it, but they were invariably smothered by the deadweight of formula. The idea seemed to be that cinema being a popular medium it should only lightly divert and not seriously engage the audience. That it was possible for a film to do both seems not to have struck them at all.

And yet Bengal never lacked craftsmen. There were excellent cameramen, editors and sound recordists who knew their jobs, and above all acting talent of a high order. If the mannerisms of the stage occasionally crept into a film performance, it was because the material itself was conceived in theatrical terms. Such mannerisms were actually encouraged as a sop to the public. Having worked with stage actors myself, I know how well they are able to tailor their style to suit the needs of cinema.

But all this excellent material was being used by people who were determined not to encroach into areas which would endanger the safety of their positions. What was singularly lacking was the spirit of adventure. Everyone played safe, and the result was stagnation.

Two years before the film society was born, I had illustrated an abridged edition of *Pather Panchali*. It had struck me then that there was a film in the book. But it was no more than a passing thought. But ever since then, whenever I read a work of Bengali fiction, half of my mind would be engaged in exploring its cinematic possibilities.

One such work of fiction was Rabindranath's *Ghare Baire*. I was then working as an artist in a British advertising agency. In my spare time, I occasionally wrote screenplays as a hobby. In the late 1940s, I wrote one of *Ghare Baire*, and there came an exciting point when a producer liked it enough to decide to sponsor a film of it. I signed a contract with him, and so did my friend Harisadhan Das Gupta, who was to direct the film. Since my contribution ended with the writing it didn't affect my job in any way.

But the producer went on to have second thoughts on the screenplay, and suggested some changes. In my youthful pride, I put my foot down. I was certainly not going to let a compromise sully my maiden contribution to cinema. This led to a deadlock and ended up in the project falling through. I felt like a pricked balloon at the time, but I can say now, after thirty-five years, that I consider it the greatest good fortune that the film was never made. Reading the screenplay now, I can see how pitifully superficial and Hollywoodish it was.

At any rate, I found my mind turning back to *Pather Panchali*, which had by then taken a more concrete shape. I pondered on it, and on the implications of giving up my job. I felt it would be fun to be an independent artist, working to satisfy a creative urge rather than satisfy the needs of a client. Even at best, advertising art is a functional art, its sole aim being to sell a product. Of course, there is a commodity aspect to films too: the film-maker works for a sponsor who expects to get his money back, and with a profit. But *if*—and this was a big if—in spite of a sponsor, it was possible to make a film in total freedom, the choice for me would be simple.

Two things happened around this time to ease the way towards a resolution.

The first was the encounter with a director of world stature.

Jean Renoir had come to Calcutta to scout locations and interview actors for a film he would be making in Bengal. Renoir was a French director who had emigrated to Hollywood just before Hitler's army invaded France. I knew his American films, but not his French ones. His films had a poetry and a humanism one rarely found in American films.

As it turned out, the man himself was very much like his films. He was genial, warm hearted, and ready with advice to a young aspirant. On two occasions, I was lucky enough to be with him while he was out looking for locations. He reacted with gasps of surprise and delight at details which eventually found their way into his film, capturing the Bengal countryside as it had never been captured before. As Renoir told me: 'You don't have to have too many elements in a film, but whatever you do, must be the right elements, the expressive elements.' A simple-sounding advice which nevertheless touched on one of the fundamentals of art, which is economy of expression.

The second important event took place a year later. I was on my first trip to London to work for a spell in the head office of our advertising agency. The first film I saw in London was De Sica's *Bicycle Thieves*. I came out of the theatre my mind fully made up. I would become a film-maker. As soon as I got back home, I would go all out to find a sponsor for *Pather Panchali*. The prospect of giving up a safe job didn't daunt me any more. I would make my film exactly as De Sica had made his: working with non-professional actors, using modest resources, and shooting on actual locations. The village which Bibhuti Bhushan had so lovingly described would be a living backdrop to the film, just as the outskirts of Rome were for De Sica's film.

Bicycle Thieves was in many ways a revelation. I assume many of you have seen the film. For those who haven't, I shall give the briefest outline of the story. Ricci, a poor worker in Rome, needs a bicycle in order to get a job. His own bike had been lying in a pawn shop. To get it back, Ricci has to pawn some household possessions. Within a day of his acquiring it, the bike is stolen. Ricci desperately tries to retrieve it, but fails. At the end of an exhausting day, in a mood of abject despair, Ricci notices a bike left standing in an apparently deserted street. After a long fight with his conscience, he decides to steal it. But he makes a clumsy job of it, and is caught and beaten up by an angry mob in the presence of his ten-year-old son Bruno. As Ricci makes his way home, weeping in humiliation, Bruno, who is also crying, joins him and offers his hand in sympathy. The two walk hand in hand and are lost in the crowd.

As you can see, there isn't much of a story, and not much of a theme either. But De Sica and his writer Zavattini pack into its ninety minutes such an incredible amount of social observation that one never notices the slenderness of the plot. The film simply bristles with details, some of which add depth to the story in unexpected ways. For instance, there's a scene towards the end where Ricci suddenly runs into the thief in front of the latter's house, pounces upon him, and demands that he hand back his bike. Hotly denying his guilt, the thief suddenly goes into an epileptic fit. As he sinks to the ground shaking and foaming at the mouth, his mother, who's been watching from an upstairs window, tosses pillows to put under his head. Meanwhile, Bruno has dragged along a policeman, whom Ricci now takes into the house to make a search. We see the miserable pigeonhole of a room where the mother cooks a meagre meal for the family of four. 'Instead of accusing him,' she says, 'why don't you find him a job?' The bike, however, is not found. As Ricci comes out of the house, he finds that the whole neighbourhood has turned against him. His hopes dashed to the ground, he has no choice but to walk despondently away.

Apart from adding dimension to the story, the film challenges our stock response of instant antipathy towards a character who brings misery on the hero by an unsocial act. But so finely is the balance maintained that the incident doesn't lessen the calamity of the hero's loss. It merely makes the film a far richer experience than a conventional treatment would have done.

One quality which is sure to be found in a great work of cinema is the revelation of large truths in small details. The world reflected in a dewdrop will serve as a metaphor for this quality. There is a scene in *Bicycle Thieves* where father and son go feverishly looking for a man they believe to have connections with the thief. In the process the two lose each other. Finding himself alone in a backstreet of a quiet neighbourhood, Bruno is seen to approach a wall while unbuttoning his pants. But before he can do what he wishes to do, Ricci suddenly appears and calls out urgently. Bruno whirls round and runs to join his father, his urge unsatisfied. This one detail brings home the implications of this desperate, day-long search more vividly than anything else. It is such details, combined with acute social observation, and the suffusing warmth of the father-and-son relationship that make *Bicycle Thieves* a great work of cinema.

I Had Set My Mind on Breaking All Manner of Conventions

When I finally decided to become a film-maker, I was well aware that I would be up against a relatively backward audience. And yet I had set my mind on breaking all manner of conventions.

I had discussed the project with a number of professionals, and, to a man, they had discouraged me by saying that it couldn't be done the way we wanted to do it. 'You can't shoot entirely on location,' they had said. 'You need the controlled conditions of a studio.' 'You can't shoot in cloudy weather; you can't shoot in the rain; you can't shoot with amateur actors,' and so on and so forth.

So one of the first things we did was to borrow a 16mm camera and go to a village and take test shots. Subrata, who was to be my cameraman, and I went to Bibhuti Bhushan's village Gopalnagar, the Nishchindipur of *Pather Panchali*. It was in the middle of the rainy season, and we had to squelch through knee-deep mud to reach our destination. But once we got there, we lost no time. We took shots in the dim light of a mango grove, we shot in pouring rain, and we shot in the falling light of dusk. Everything came out.

I shall not go into the various ordeals we had to face in the two-and-a-half years it took to make *Pather Panchali*. The story has been told often enough. But what I have probably not mentioned elsewhere is that it was in a way a blessing that the film took so long to make. We learnt film-making as we went along, and since we went on for so long, it gave us that much more time to learn.

With all my knowledge of Western cinema, the first thing I realized was that none of the films I had ever seen was remotely like the story I was about to film. *Pather Panchali* had its roots deep in the soil of Bengal. The life it described had its own pace and its own rhythm, which in turn had to mould the pace and the rhythm of the film. The inspiration had to come from the book, and from the real surroundings in which we had decided to place the story.

If the books on film-making helped, it was only in a general sort of way. For instance, none of them tells you how to handle an actor who has never faced a camera before. You had to devise your own method. You had to find out yourself how to catch the hushed stillness of dusk in a Bengali village, when the wind drops and turns the ponds into sheets of glass, dappled by the leaves of shaluk and shapla, and the smoke from ovens settles in wispy trails over the landscape, and the plaintive blows on conch shells from homes far and near are joined by the chorus of crickets, which rises as the light falls, until all one sees are the stars in the sky, and the stars that blink and swirl in the thickets.

We wanted to show fireflies in *Aparajito*. The books didn't tell us that the light they gave off was too weak to be photographed. Our own tests with the camera proved that. So we had to invent a way of showing them. What we did was photograph a group of bare-bodied assistants in black loin cloths, who hopped about in total darkness, holding in their hands tiny electric bulbs which flashed on and off in a simulation of the dance of the fireflies.

If film books didn't help much, I was helped enormously by Bibhuti Bhushan. He is one writer whose stories are a gold mine of cinematic observation, and it is fortunate that I developed a taste for him right at the start of my career. Even in his lesser works—and there aren't many that rise to the heights of *Pather Panchali* and *Aranyak*—his eye and ear produce marvels of observation. I shall give one example. It comes from the well-known short story 'Puinmacha'.

Annapurna's daughter Khenti has just got married, and it is now time for the bride to depart. The palki is resting on the ground with the bride and the groom in it. Annapurna, whose heart is torn by anguish, glances at the palki and notices—I translate—'that the end of Khenti's modest red baluchari has trailed out of the palki, and is nestling against a drooping cluster of medi flowers by the bamboo fencing'.

In its context, this is a heart-rending detail, and a perfect film close-up of the kind described by Eisenstein as 'pars pro toto', part standing for the whole.

Yet another quality which Bibhuti Bhushan had was a wonderful ear for lifelike speech. A vital and unending pursuit for a film-maker is the study of speech patterns: speech as a reflection of class, and speech as revealing states of mind. This is one area where Bengali cinema had been particularly weak. The 1940s and 1950s were the era of something called smart dialogue. One often heard it said that 'so-and-so is unsurpassed as a writer of smart dialogue'.

The implication seemed to be that dialogue was something to be admired for its own sake and not, as it should be, as a concomitant of the characters who speak it. The epitome of this was, of course, *Udayer Pathay*, where the hero's speech gave the impression that he was born spouting epigrams. The best film dialogue is where one doesn't feel the presence of the writer at all. I am talking here of the kind of film that tries to capture the feel of reality. There are also films which attempt a larger-than-life style, or an oblique, fractured or expressionist style: I myself wrote dialogue with end rhymes in *Hirok Rajar Deshe*, which was a fantasy. But the overwhelming majority of narrative films belong in the tradition of realism, where the dialogue sustains the feeling of lifelikeness that is conveyed through the camera.

This realism in films is not the naturalism of the painter who sets up his easel before his subject and proceeds to record faithfully what he sees. For a film-maker, there is no ready-made reality which he can straightaway capture on film. What surrounds him is only raw material. He must at all times use this material selectively. Objects, locales, people, speech, viewpoints—everything must be carefully chosen, to serve the ends of his story. In other words, creating reality is part of the creative process, where the imagination is aided by the eye and the ear.

The novelist too has a similar task. In his supposed omniscience, he can describe the innermost workings of his characters' minds, while evoking the surroundings in the minutest details. The reader sees only what the author chooses to describe. It may be just a factual description, or it may go beyond that, where the author adds his subjective comments to it. It is such description and such comments—a combination of the concrete and the abstract—that builds up the picture of reality in the reader's mind.

A film, on the other hand, presents information in lumps, as it were. At any given moment, the image on the screen may be filled with a plethora of details, each carrying information. In other words, the language here is far more diffused than the language of words, and it is the film-maker's job to direct the attention of the audience to the dominant idea contained in the image.

If the idea is conveyed through dialogue, there is usually no ambiguity. But when it is conveyed in non-verbal terms—through gestures, objects, pure sounds, and so on—precise communication becomes difficult. When a writer is at a loss for words, he can turn to his thesaurus; but there is no thesaurus for the film-maker. He can of course fall back on clichés—goodness knows how many films have used the snuffed-out candle to suggest death—but the really effective language is both fresh and vivid at the same time, and the search for it an inexhaustible one.

It's Not Just What You Say, But How You Say It

Since nine out of ten Bengali films are based on novels, and since both films and novels use words and images, one would think that such novels would substantially help in the creation of a film language. But here a problem arises. I don't know if it is a reflection of the Bengali temperament, but many of our writers seem more inclined to use their minds, rather than their eyes and ears. In other words, there is a marked tendency to avoid concrete observation. Here is a small segment of Balzac's description of Madame Vauquer's lodging house in *Old Goriot*:

> The indestructible furniture which every other house throws out, finds its way to the lodging house, for the same reason that the human wreckage of civilization drifts to the hospitals for the incurable. In the room, you would find a barometer with a monk, which appears when it is wet; execrable engravings, bad enough to spoil your appetite, and all framed with unvarnished black wood; a clock with a tortoise-shell case inlaid with copper; a green stove; lamps coated with dust and oil; a long table covered with oil cloth so greasy that a facetious boarder can write his name on it with fingernails; broken-backed chairs; wretched little grass mats unravelling endlessly, without ever coming completely to pieces; and finally, miserable foot warmers, their orifices enlarged by decay, their hinges broken and their wood charred. The furniture is all old, cracked, decaying, shaky, worm-eaten, decrepit, rickety, ramshackle and on its last leg.

Here you have the art director's job already done for him. This sort of vivid observation—the kind that is a godsend to a film-maker—is by no means common in Bengali fiction. Bankim reveals this quality occasionally—there is a minutely observed description of Nagendranath's house in *Bisha Briksha*, and Debi Choudhurani's houseboat is described in sumptuous detail. Such descriptions occur in almost every page of *Hutom*, and in more recent times, one finds it again and again in the writings of Kamal Kumar Majumdar. But to come to a major novel I'm involved in at the moment, for the second time—Rabindranath's *Ghare Baire*—such concreteness is noticeably lacking.

For instance, there is no description of Nikhilesh's house anywhere in the book. Of the two rooms where most of the action takes place—Nikhilesh's bedroom in the inner part of the house and the drawing room in the outer part—barely three or four details are mentioned by name. Sandip has regular meetings with his boys, but we are never told where they meet. Occasionally, there is a description of what Bimala is wearing, but none of the male characters' dresses are ever described.

In the present case, this lack of visualization may be because the author himself is not the chronicler, but the three main characters who by turns reveal their minds and motives and advance the story. Also, the clash of ideas and ideals which forms the substance of the novel may account for the predominance of the abstract over the concrete. However, the fact remains that the trait is a common one in Bengali fiction, and leads one to conclude that the writers are either incapable of or disinclined to visualize beyond a certain point. This itself need not be held against a novel, but in a film writer, the tendency can only lead to a film that shows a lot, but tells very little. A film by its very nature makes the characters and their surroundings concrete. The camera makes them so. You *see* the characters, you *see* where they live, you *see* the setting in which the story unfolds. But this concreteness is a sum of the elements that go to make a character, a room, a background;

and these can come alive only through a deliberate and apt choice of such elements. In other words, what a film says is intimately bound up with these elements, these visual details.

Our films have consistently neglected these details in their preoccupation with content. Our critics too have shown a tendency to judge a film predominantly on what it says rather than how it says it. I have no wish to belittle content, but we must remember that the lousiest of films have been made on the loftiest of themes. That a director says all the right things is in itself no guarantee of artistry. At best it is a reflection of his attitude, or his ideology. If it is a true reflection—and often there is no way of telling—it will mark him out as an honest man, but not necessarily as an artist. Unless a film aims at deliberate obfuscation, or is unintelligible through sheer clumsiness of execution, what it says is usually clear to all. But what it says is only a partial index of a film-maker's personality, because it is the manner of saying which indicates the artist. There are film-makers who are not overly concerned with what they say as long as they can say it with style or finesse. One would sooner describe them as craftsmen, because it is difficult to think of an artist who is totally devoid of an attitude to life and society which he reveals in his work. Usually, the attitude is implicit in his choice of material. But his success in portraying it in terms of cinema is in direct ratio to the purity, power, and freshness of his language.

I shall end this talk by describing a scene from one of my own films, which attempts to use a language entirely free from literary and theatrical influences. Except for one line of dialogue in its seven minutes, the scene says what it has to say in terms that speak to the eye and the ear. The scene will also introduce an important element I haven't spoken of so far. This is the recurring motif. Appearing at several points in a film, often in different contexts, these motifs serve as unifying elements.

The seven minutes refer to the opening scene of *Charulata*. Once again I assume many of you will have seen the film—if not in the theatres, at least on television. This scene establishes visually the approximate period of the story, the upper-class ambience in which the story unfolds, the central character of Charu, and a crucial aspect of her relationship with her husband. In other words, it sets the stage for the drama that follows. I should point out that no such scene as this occurs in *Nastaneer*, the Rabindranath story on which the film is based, and that there are elements in it which have been invented for the purpose of the film. But this is inevitable in any adaptation of a literary work for the screen. It is also justifiable if what has been introduced serves to articulate the author's theme, and illuminates the characters conceived by him.

The film opens with the letter 'B' being embroidered on a handkerchief by Charu. This will prove to be a major motif in the film. We will learn later that the handkerchief is meant for Charu's husband Bhupati. It will trigger off the conversation which will make Bhupati aware of Charu's loneliness. Towards the end of the film, after Bhupati's traumatic discovery of Charu's feelings towards Amal, Bhupati will use the handkerchief to wipe his tears, and will notice the embroidery before he decides to return to his wife.

As Charu finishes her needlework, we hear the grandfather clock in the veranda strike four. The clock is heard chiming the hour at several points in the film, and may be said to be the second motif.

But what is special about four o'clock? We learn in a few moments when Charu puts down the embroidery, goes out of the bedroom and down the veranda to the top of the backstairs, calls out to the servant and asks him to take tea to the master in the office. We thus know that Bhupati's place of work is in the house itself.

Her duty done, Charu comes back to the bedroom. For a few moments she is undecided what to do. This, of course, is an inevitable aspect of boredom. One has time on one's hand, but is frequently at a loss to know how to use it. Charu briefly admires her handiwork, then picks up a book from the bed, riffles through the pages and puts it down.

She now comes out of the bedroom, and once again proceeds down the veranda towards the outer apartments. Apart from the obvious fact of Charu's restlessness, these movements in and out of rooms help to establish the plan of the first floor of Bhupati's house where most of the action will take place. In a story like *Charulata*, the setting itself is a character, and must be established carefully in all its details as any human participant in the story.

Charu now comes into the drawing room and picks out from a bookcase a novel by Bankimchandra. This is the third motif: Bankim will prove to be a common link between Charu and Amal.

Charu has already reacted to a monkey man's drumming which is heard from somewhere in the neighbourhood. Idly turning the pages of the novel, she makes her way to her husband's study which lies in the direction of the sound of drumming. She goes to a window in the room, raises the shutters and peers out—and there is the monkey man in the house next door.

This gives Charu an idea. She scurries out of the room, comes back to the bedroom and takes out a lorgnette from a drawer. This lorgnette is the fourth motif, and will feature in a crucial scene with Amal later.

As she hurries back to her husband's study, swinging the lorgnette in her hand, the camera follows the object through the veranda railings. Precisely, the same viewpoint will recur in a very different context when a triumphant Charu will make a headlong dash for Amal's room, this time swinging in her hand the magazine which has published her article.

The monkey man is now brought up close as Charu observes him through the lorgnette. But the man goes away and Charu now turns to another window. This one gives on the street. This time Charu has a glimpse of a palki, which is followed by a fat man who carries a pot of sweetmeats dangling at the end of a string. The man goes out of view, but Charu, anxious to stay with this amusing character a little longer, rushes to the drawing room and follows him through three successive windows until the man turns a corner and is finally lost to sight.

It was important to stress this playful aspect of Charu because this is where she is farthest from her staid husband and closest to the youthful, exuberant Amal.

Charu has now reached a point where she is once again undecided what to do.

The first musical motif is introduced here: a line of melody which will be associated with Charu, and which now unfolds as Charu makes her way pensively to the piano. She lifts the lid and casually strikes a note. But she is immediately distracted by the sound of booted footsteps from the veranda.

We now see Bhupati in his shirtsleeves, stomping busily down the veranda towards the bedroom.

Charu comes out of the drawing room and stands by the

door, looking the way her husband has gone, her chin resting on the hand holding the lorgnette. She knows her husband will return, and sure enough he does, this time with a fat book in his hand, his eyes glued to an open page.

He stops by Charu for a moment to turn a page, then walks on without noticing her. Charu keeps looking at the receding figure. Then, in a playful gesture, she brings the lorgnette up to her eyes. For a brief moment Bhupati is brought up close before he goes out of sight down the staircase.

Charu removes the lorgnette from her eyes and keeps looking for a few more seconds towards the door through which her husband has just gone out.

Then her hand with the lorgnette flops down.

We now know that Charu is resigned to her state of loneliness. And this brings the scene to a close.

2

The Making of a Film: Structure, Language and Style

Even today, there are debates over whether or not cinema can be called a form of art. Those who are not prepared to give it that status claim that cinema has no soul of its own; it is a weird mixture of components taken from literature and other forms of art.

The problem is over the word 'art'. If the word 'language' is used instead, I think the true nature of cinema will become clearer and there will be no need for debate.

Just as a writer has words at his disposal, a film-maker has image and sound that make up the language of cinema. If this language is not handled skilfully, if the film-maker fails to grasp its grammar and if, in the end, the final message of the film is not imparted strongly enough, how can anyone ever produce a good film? So much is written every day, but how much of that emerges as good literature? The artist must come before his art. Where there is no artist, no art can be created even if all the relevant material is available.

There is no doubt that cinema includes elements of literature and other forms of art. The conflict shown in drama, the narrative description in a novel to establish its plot and

---

'Chalachitra Rachona: Aangik, Bhasha O Bhongee', *Chalachitra*, Annual Issue, 1959.

set its atmosphere, the interplay between light and shade in a painting, the movement and rhythm of music—each has found a place in cinema. But the language that consists of image and sound—which has no existence unless it is seen and heard—is a completely distinct language. As a result, even when the message being conveyed is the same, there is bound to be a difference in style. That style is exclusive to cinema. That is why, even when it bears elements from other art forms, cinema remains unique.

Image and sound. An image here is not just a picture. It is a picture that speaks. In other words, the picture does not begin and end in itself, the way a painting does. What matters chiefly here is the meaning of that image. Every image is like a whole sentence, and the sum total of all the images is the final message of a film. Even in the silent era, images carried meanings. Their language was not dependent on dialogue.

And sound? Sound complements image. One has no meaning without the other. It is not possible to understand the language of cinema unless one keeps both one's eyes and ears open. If a scene does not have any sound, even its absence can convey a special meaning. Silence itself becomes its message.

Just as a writer's works can be classified into different categories according to his chosen subject and style, so can a film-maker's. Cinema has used novels, poetry and drama as well as educational narrative. In this particular discussion, we shall focus on only one category—films based on novels and stories. That is what is best known, the world's most outstanding films fall into this category.

The process of film-making can be divided into three phases. The first is writing the scenario. The second phase involves either selecting an appropriate location based on the scenario or building a set, getting together enough actors to play the characters as described in the scenario, and shooting the whole process. In the third phase, all the shots, taken piecemeal, are arranged in the same order in which they appear in the scenario. This third phase is called editing. A scenario is the basic structure of a film. It describes in words what, on the screen, is expressed through image and sound. It is this structure that the actors lean on when they follow the director's instructions and work together to make a film come alive and give it a cohesive form. That is why a scenario cannot be treated with indifference. If it has drawbacks and weaknesses, those are bound to be reflected in the main body of the film, no matter how masterly the direction. Equally, even if a scenario is well written, one cannot relax completely, since weak and faulty direction may well ruin a perfectly good scenario.

The use of equipment and gadgets is inevitable in every phase of film-making, except when the scenario is being written. Cinema speaks a language that belongs essentially to our age of machines. If a gadget called a camera had not been invented, such a language would certainly not have come into being. When sound began to be added to image and silent films gave way to the talkies, it was because of the invention of sound recording machines.

Once images and sounds have been recorded with the help of a camera and sound recording machine, one must turn to all the equipment in a laboratory to develop and print the whole thing. Then the editor has the responsibility of running repeatedly the various pieces of recorded image and sound through a machine called Moviola, making a distinction between the 'good' and the 'bad' portions, using a pair of scissors to cut out the 'bad' or unnecessary bits and rejoining the good portions with film-cement. In the final phase comes background music. What is played on musical instruments is recorded on a sound recording machine. Then a re-recording machine has to be used to fit it in with spoken words and other sounds, without disturbing the impact or balance of either. It is only when this last most complex task is finished that one may be free of gadgets.

Needless to say, if the operators of these machines work like machines themselves, i.e. if they do not possess an adequate aesthetic sense, it can hamper the making of a good film.

Those who see films—and who doesn't?—will have noticed that instead of being shown from the same angle throughout, a scene is broken into different parts and various parts are then shown from different angles. Each individual part is called a 'shot'. This system of breaking up a scene is unique to cinema. No other art form requires such a system. It is not based on a film-maker's whim, and its sole aim is not just to create variety in the presentation of a scene. It has an artistic purpose as well as linguistic merit.

Such purpose and merit may be explained if a particular excerpt from a scenario is analysed shot by shot. That will also explain the problems, big and small, that film-making entails. Naturally, no great, widely applicable theory is going to emerge from discussing these instances. Like other forms of art, cinema does not have cut-and-dried theories or formulae. The style adopted in a film is inevitably dictated by the story itself, and the views and attitudes of the director. It goes without saying that the same scene in the same story will appear different if handled by a different director with variations in the use of film language.

As an example, a sequence from *Pather Panchali* may be discussed. Bibhuti Bhushan described it in his novel like this:

He got out at the nearest station and walked to his village. By the time he got there it was early evening. He met few people on the way; those that he did, he ignored and hurried towards home with an anxious heart. As he passed through the main entrance, he said to himself, 'Oh look at that bamboo grove! It's leaning right over the wall. Bhuvan kaka is never going to have it chopped—what a bother!' Then he stepped into the courtyard and called eagerly, as was his wont: 'O Ma Durga . . . Apu!'

The sound of his voice brought Sarbajaya out of her room. Harihar smiled and said, 'Is everything all right? Where have the children gone? Aren't they home?'

Sarbajaya stepped forward quietly and removed the heavy bundle from Harihar's hand. 'Come inside,' she said. Harihar noticed that his wife was unusually quiet, but that caused him no alarm. His imagination was running in a different direction altogether—his children would come rushing in a minute. Durga would ask, 'What's in there, Baba?' and Harihar would surprise everyone by quickly untying the bundle and taking out a sari for Durga, *alta* for her feet, a couple of books and a toy train made of tin. 'I have brought you a new rolling pin and board,' he said as he walked into his room. 'It is made with wood from a jackfruit tree.' Then he cast a somewhat disappointed glance round the room and said, 'Apu? Durga? Are they both out?'

Sarbajaya could no longer control herself. 'Durga? She is no more . . . no more with us . . . she left us all!' she wailed loudly. 'Where were you all this while?'

***

The above event was described in the scenario of *Pather Panchali* in the following manner:

1. A cloudy day. A track going through a field.
    Long-shot: Apu, wearing a dark shawl and holding an
    empty bottle of kerosene, goes down the track far into
    the distance.

    (Background music)

    Dissolve to

2. Cloudy day. The small veranda attached to Indir's room.
    Close-up: Rice is being cooked in a pot placed over a clay
    stove. It is bubbling furiously, almost boiling over. The
    lid over the pot is moving up and down. Tilt up:
    Sarbajaya's face. She is squatting, her cheek resting on
    her right hand. The look in her eyes is distant, unblinking.

    (Background music continues)

3. Cloudy day. The courtyard in Sarbajaya's house.
    Mid-shot: A girl of about twelve (Bini) enters through a
    door that leads out of the courtyard, carrying a basket
    of vegetables in her hand.
    She comes and stands next to the veranda. (Sarbajaya
    cannot be seen in this shot.)
    Bini: Notun khurima!

    (Background music continues)

4. Cloudy day. Indir's veranda, as seen from the courtyard.
    Mid-shot: In the foreground, to the right, is Bini with her
    back to the camera. To the left, at some distance, Sarbajaya
    is still sitting in the same position, her back to Bini.
    Bini: Notun khurima!
    Sarbajaya does not answer.
    Bini: Ma sent all this stuff. I'm keeping it over here.
    Bini places the basket on the veranda.

    (Background music continues)

5. Cloudy day.
   Close-shot: Having put the basket down, Bini moves back towards the door, glancing at Sarbajaya.

                              (Background music fades out)

   Dissolve to

6. Cloudy day. Bamboo grove behind Harihar's house.
   Long top-shot: Harihar is seen walking in the distance.
   Harihar: Apu!

7. Cloudy day. Indir's veranda.
   Close-up: Sarbajaya's reaction upon hearing Harihar's voice—her cheek moves slightly away from her hand and her bangle slides a little down her arm.

8. Cloudy day. Harihar is by the compound wall on the southern side.
   Mid-shot: Harihar stops suddenly. A branch from a mango tree has fallen across the wall and broken a portion of it.
   Harihar (to himself): Couldn't you have waited a little longer?
   Harihar steps over the fallen branch and moves on. The camera pans with him.
   He faces his broken home and stares at it for a few seconds. Then he passes through a door and goes out of the frame. The camera stops panning. A cow can be seen on the other side of the damaged wall, chewing the cud in its broken shed. Behind the cowshed is Harihar's veranda.
   (In the background is the sound of Harihar opening a door.)
   After a while, a long-shot shows him near his veranda. He casts anxious glances everywhere.
   Harihar (anxiously): Khoka! Durga!

Sarbajaya passes him and climbs a few steps onto the veranda.

Harihar: Oh, you're home!

Sarbajaya: Come in . . .

Harihar starts climbing the steps.

9. Cloudy day. Harihar's veranda.

Mid-shot: Having reached the veranda, Harihar places his tin attaché-case and a bundle on the floor. Then he massages his wrists and wipes his face with one end of his dhoti.

Harihar: How are you?

Sarbajaya pours water from a small metal pot into a bigger pot for Harihar to wash his feet. Then she brings a pair of wooden clogs, a *piri* (wooden seat) and a towel and places them by the pot.

Harihar: Have those two gone out?

Sarbajaya moves towards the steps without saying a word.

Harihar puts a hand on her shoulder to stop her.

Harihar: Where are you going? Look at the things I've brought!

Sarbajaya stops. Harihar sits down to untie the knot on his bundle.

10. Cloudy day. Harihar's veranda.

Mid-close shot: Sarbajaya is in the foreground, facing the camera. Behind her is Harihar, opening his bundle.

Harihar: You think I wouldn't have come home earlier if I could? My God, I had to go *everywhere* . . . and then, when I got to Vishnupur, I finally had a stroke of luck . . . so, look, here's a picture of Lakshmi, just like you said. And I had it framed, too. And here . . . these are made from jackfruit wood . . .

Harihar leaves the rolling pin and picks up a striped sari, offering it to Sarbajaya.

Harihar: And look . . .!

11. Cloudy day.
    Close-up: A striped sari for Durga.
    Harihar's voice: It's for Durga.
    Sarbajaya's hand clutches the sari tightly. Then her hand moves upward, and the camera tilts up.
    Sarbajaya's face is distorted with pain and tears. Her hand moves to her mouth, she catches the sari between her teeth and sits down, still crying.
    (Instead of the sound of her sobbing, a taar-shehnai plays at a high pitch.)

12. Cloudy day.
    Mid-close-shot (same angle as 10):
    Sarbajaya is sitting on the veranda. Harihar bends over her, extremely anxious.
    Sarbajaya falls from her sitting position and is prostrate on the floor.

                        (Shehnai in the background)

13. Cloudy day.
    Close-shot: Sarbajaya is lying on the floor, sobbing. Harihar shakes her by the shoulder, as if to say: What's the matter? What's wrong?
    Sarbajaya shakes her head, to indicate that Durga is no more. The camera tracks forward to move towards Harihar's face.
    Harihar has finally grasped the situation. He tries to get to his feet, looking dazed, but sits down at once, bending over and crying. The camera tracks back to its original position.

Harihar wails: Durga! Durga Ma!

>   (Shehnai in the background)

14. The pond behind Harihar's house.

    Mid-shot: Apu is standing there, a full bottle of kerosene in his hand.

    Harihar (in the background): Durga Ma!

    Apu continues to stand like a statue—stunned and helpless. The camera tracks forward quickly to catch Apu's face. Fade out.

>   (Shehnai fades out)

***

The events in the screenplay, spanning a whole year starting from Apu's first day in school to Durga's death, had been divided according to different seasons. Durga gets caught in the rain in late March and falls ill. Every scene from that event to Harihar's return was shot on a cloudy day. It is not as if the sun didn't come out between showers, but in this portion of the novel, the mood is heavy and dismal throughout. That could be captured in the film only if the scenes were shot on cloudy days. The total length of the sequence is five minutes.

It took us three days to complete the shooting, and every shot had to be taken two or three times. That is normal practice when a film is being made.

Let us now consider the shots in detail.

1. Long-shot: Every shot is given a name, depending on the distance between the camera and the object on which it is focussed. If a person's face is shown, from his chin to his head (or less), it is called a 'big close-up'. From head to waist is 'close-up', and up to the legs is 'mid-shot'. Beyond that is 'mid-long-shot' and 'long-shot'.

    The first long-shot was taken against an open field in

order to highlight Apu's loneliness and vulnerability. Only a year before, Apu was seen walking down the same track to go to his school, holding Durga's hand. Durga's absence strikes the audience even more forcefully.

2. There is a time difference between this shot and the preceding one. In order to capture that, 'dissolve' was used. What happens in 'dissolve' is that one image fades out gradually and another takes its place. If the camera moves from one shot to another directly, without fading out, that technique is called 'cut'. The execution of a 'dissolve' naturally takes a little longer than a 'cut'.

   The movement on the lid on the rice pot and the distant look in Sarbajaya's eyes would not have been easily noticeable unless they could be seen from close quarters; hence we decided to use a close-up. After the wide expanse of the field in the previous shot, the sudden contraction in this close-up helped to continue with the same sad mood, yet created a difference in its rhythm.

   A camera can be moved up and down, or from one side to another. The first is called 'tilting', and the second 'panning'.

   In this particular shot, I thought I could draw a simple parallel between the boiling rice covered by a lid and Sarbajaya's grief and other pent-up emotions bubbling inside her.

3. The main aim behind bringing Bini into this scene was to show that Sarbajaya's neighbours were helping her during this difficult time.

   Bini first appears in a mid-shot. When she walks over to the veranda the shot changes almost to a close-up. Bini gets no answer from Sarbajaya when she calls out to her. We do not know how Sarbajaya has reacted to Bini's arrival since we cannot see Sarbajaya in this shot; nor is it possible to gauge the distance between her and Bini.

The next shot follows to satisfy our curiosity on both those counts.

4. This shot shows Sarbajaya and Bini together (two-shot), which clarifies their positions. There is quite a lot of distance between them, but because both have to be shown at the same time, a mid-long-shot has to be used. Sarbajaya does not respond to Bini's call—that indicates the depth of her grief.

Bini's face cannot be seen in this shot. But we are curious to know how she reacts to Sarbajaya's somewhat unnatural behaviour. What it means is that the camera has to change its angle and move to Bini's face. The moment of going from one shot to another has to be carefully chosen.

5. The shot changes in the middle of Bini putting the basket down. The first shot shows her beginning to do so, and the second shows what happens next. While shooting this scene, both shots took in the entire action of the basket being placed on the veranda. Later, the editor deleted the extra portion where necessary.

The advantage in choosing that particular moment to go from one shot to another is that the audience is so busy watching the movement of the basket that no one notices when the camera changes its angle.

A director has to take care that the audience does not see through the ploys employed in film-making involving equipment and gadgets. Skilful editing helps, to a great extent, to keep these ploys hidden.

The look in Bini's eyes and the way she steps back imply that she is taken aback, perhaps even a little scared.

6. There is another dissolve between this shot and the

preceding one. The dissolve simply means that soon after Bini's departure, Harihar will be seen walking to his house.

The audience is naturally waiting eagerly for the dramatic moment when Harihar will be told about his daughter's death. This shot gives us the chance to inform the audience that Harihar is on his way, thereby delaying that moment and adding to the overall dramatic effect.

A long-shot was taken from a sixteen-foot-high bamboo platform to show Harihar walking down a path through a bamboo grove. There is no background music in this shot, which automatically creates a somewhat eerie silence. There is no sound at all; it is as if the whole of nature is holding its breath for that final tragic moment.

The silence is broken by Harihar calling out affectionately to his children. Has Sarbajaya heard him call?

7. She has. How should she react? Her emotions cannot be exaggerated since the tears she has held back cannot break free so easily. That is why a slight movement is needed, and so a close-up is required. Sarbajaya's cheek up to now was pressed against a white bangle. Now her hand moves and the bangle slips down by an inch. That is enough, since, until now, she has been shown sitting perfectly still. The jerky movement of the bangle is a reflection of the sudden tumult in her heart. Where is Harihar now?

8. He is by their compound wall. The state of the wall prompts him to make a remark to himself—it conveys regret but does not say anything more than is necessary (unlike the novel which has a lot of additional words). The drama intensifies. Harihar seems to think that the destruction of his house is the biggest tragedy he must deal with.

This shot was made to last nearly a minute and a half in order to delay the moment of truth. There was no 'event' as such—the only action showed the cow chewing the cud. It was like the lull before a storm.

When the shot begins, Harihar is in a mid-shot. By the time it ends, he has walked away from the camera and gone into a long-shot.

As he starts to climb the steps onto the veranda, we wait until he is halfway there before changing the shot and . . .

9. . . . reaching the top of the veranda. Since the first shot shows him climbing the first two steps, and the second catches him going up the remaining two, the change from one angle to another does not jar. This shot contains Harihar's questions and haphazard remarks, as well as Sarbajaya's prolonged action—pouring water, bringing a *piri*, a towel and the clogs—which serve to test the audience's patience even further. When and how would Harihar be given the terrible news?

10. The shot changes as soon as Harihar starts to untie his bundle. Now Sarbajaya's face is visible, but it is not yet time for a close-up.

Harihar does not show her Durga's sari at once. He brings out two other objects before reaching out for the sari.

11. Now we come to the sari. This is the right moment for a close-up. Harihar has brought a sari for Durga, but she is no more. Harihar does not know that. So—quite unperturbed—he offers it to Sarbajaya. Will Sarbajaya be able to maintain the enormous self-control that has so far kept her from breaking down?

The sound of wailing has an element of horror in it. In order to avoid that, instead of the natural sounds of Sarbajaya crying, we played a sad tune on a taar-shehnai, using the raga called Patadeep. It was as effective as a wail. I believe the pathos in this scene deepened further with the music.

12. Apart from music, no other sound is used in this shot.

13. The camera moves closer to Harihar's face to focus on the moment of his realization. As soon as Harihar breaks down, the purpose of this shot is almost over. But instead of ending the scene here, an extra shot was added.

14. The scene began with Apu—and so it ends with him.

The final shot was taken much later than the others. But since its mood was identical to the mood in the previous shot, the sudden appearance of Apu even before Harihar's wail could die away helped that shot to merge with the preceding one and become an intrinsic part of the whole sequence.

The fade-out at the end of the final shot implies a full stop. Image and sound (in this case, background music) fade away slowly—and after a few seconds of darkness begins a new image, a new chapter.

3

The Language of Cinema: Then and Now

In recent years, one has seen hints of some new elements in foreign films. People in our own country have also become aware of these. Some of them are related to subject matter. Various events and problems integral to human life and society are now finding room in films. Even a few years ago they were disregarded on the grounds that 'the-audience-won't-like-it' or 'cannot-show-it-in-a-film'. Details of physical relationships between men and women—though not new to art and literature—have only recently started in cinema. If someone goes to a film festival abroad, he may well end up thinking that sex is the only subject that modern films are portraying.

Another, more important, aspect of these new elements is related to a film's language. It is not as if film language has never seen a change before. Such a change can be spotted at once if one compares an American film made in the early 1930s with one made in the 1950s. However, the difference there is relatively subtle, so it may not become immediately visible. But the new style that can be seen in films today often appears to be openly aggressive in nature; the attempt to create a sensation is quite clear. The difference between old styles and

---

'Chalachitrer Bhasha: Shekaal O Ekaal', *Desh Binodan*, 1969.

the current one is so obvious that perhaps that is the reason why the influence of the latter is spreading so widely and quickly. Many young directors in Europe, America, Japan, Brazil, Argentina and various other countries are speaking this new language, shaking the audience by their shoulders time and again, and confusing the film critics. Some of the same critics have started saying that this new language is the only one suitable for cinema; any film that fails to use it is disqualified from being included among those who have created contemporary art in cinema, relevant to our times.

This is a serious matter. It is serious because the age we live in is one that simply follows trends and fashions. Even in our own poor country, the joint tyranny of these two factors has been felt. Many young Bengali men can no longer sit cross-legged because they wear thin narrow trousers and, in such trousers, it is not possible to sit in that manner. Yet if they do not wear them, they cannot keep up with the latest fashion. There is no guarantee that what applies to clothes will not also apply to art. It is therefore necessary to consider the subject of language in some detail. Is it really something that has introduced a new phase in cinema, compared to which everything we have seen so far has become old-fashioned? Or is it something like those tight trousers which cannot perform certain functions, so that those functions have to be abandoned for you to be considered fashionable enough?

II

It is not inappropriate to use the analogy of clothes when talking of language. Like clothes, language has two aspects. One of these is merely functional; all it does is express certain feelings. The other is its artistic aspect, where there is a question of sweetness, lucidity and even wit in its use. Whenever a new language is formed, it is usually just to express feelings or moods. Once that primary need has been met, it can acquire beauty and elegance in the hands of an artist. However, even when a language attains full maturity, it cannot hope to last forever because, as times change, so do a conscious artist's views and attitudes. They are bound to be reflected in his language.

Many people are aware that the language of cinema that came into being sixty years ago was a confused mixture of styles and moods found in classical art forms such as music, painting, literature and drama. The first motion picture that was shown to the general public simply showed a train pulling in at a platform. Even if the scene was shown as a still photograph, its message would have been perfectly clear. But the motion picture had a difference: the event it showed was confined to a specific period, i.e. only for as long as the image remained on the screen. As soon as we realize that, we can see that cinema has a relationship with music; and that although it shows images, cinema is different from paintings or photographs.

That shot of the train, taken by Lumiere, was no more than an ordinary daily event, devoid of a story or an element of drama. Soon afterwards, stories began to be told in films. That was when the language of cinema started to acquire its own distinct form. The man who was among the first to build on it was the extraordinarily talented American director, D.W. Griffith. The grammar of cinematic language that rests on certain techniques adopted by the camera and editing were almost all invented by Griffith. The first thing that Griffith understood was that just as a story cannot be verbally told in one breath, and, even when it is written, sentences must be arranged one after the other, a film must tell a story through various scenes which are further divided into various shots. Each shot is like a sentence or a word. It speaks just like the spoken word, but its language has essentially to do with images and visual material. But that is not all. Just as a written story has to be divided into paragraphs and chapters, a story in a film can be broken up into different segments through the use of mechanical or chemical techniques known as a 'mix' or 'fade'.

It was again Griffith who pioneered the use of different angles of the camera (which led to the birth of such terms as close-up, mid-shot, long-shot, top-shot etc) and applied it successfully to put across his message. Close-ups, in particular, were invented to capture a character's state of mind, his appearance and other details of his gestures and expression. Even today, it is impossible to make a film without using close-ups.

When close-ups arrived, a distinction between films and the theatre was clearly established in spite of the dramatic content in films, since the audience at a play could not get very close to the actors. They were fixed to their seats in the auditorium, so the distance between the actors and the audience could not change.

Cinema offers the chance to bring the actors closer to the spectators, but that is not the only reason why a camera is moved back and forth. There is an artistic need to do so, and again it was Griffith who was the first to feel that need. He could see that cinema lacked the direct contact between actors and audience that the theatre could offer. The contact in cinema was established through the camera. If we have to hear a third person describe a dramatic event, whether or not the element of drama comes through in that description depends entirely on the narrator. The camera plays the role of that narrator.

No matter what the event may be, it is the job of the camera to obey the director's instructions and relate that event in a suitable manner. The language of cinema is therefore primarily the language spoken by the camera. That is as true today as it was in Griffith's time.

Gradually, as he continued to add one shot after another to tell a story, Griffith became aware of the rhythmic aspect of a film. I have already remarked on the limited time within which a film has to make its point. What Griffith saw was that when shots of different lengths depicting different moods were put together, not only was it telling a story, it was also creating a rhythm as the story unfolded. A complex mixed rhythm was rising from the differences in the distance between the camera and the visual material, the variations in the length of each shot and the various emotions that the visual image or object could evoke. It was the same as the rhythm in a piece of music, created through the synthesis of its beat, tempo, the rise and fall of a voice, the differences in the scale used in a tune, and the mood all these could arouse.

As a result of this primary realization by Griffith, that rhythmic cinematic language—based on literature, drama, painting and music—took on quite a distinct form in the middle of the silent era, i.e. around 1915. Almost any director could learn to use its grammar and, through its use, convey his own message reasonably clearly. A few talented American and European film-makers experimented some more with this language and helped to strengthen and enrich it further.

Again, it was in Hollywood that Mack Sennet created a new language for slapstick comedy. What was no more than crude slapstick in the theatre became high-class art in cinema. Sennet, too, had realized that it was not enough to film the same satire and humour that were prevalent in the theatre.

Camera and editing techniques were certainly required to provide food for comedy, or none of it would appear particularly comic. Among the comedians who followed Sennet's footsteps and became well known, Charlie Chaplin and Buster Keaton deserve special mention.

Compassionate and socially aware, Chaplin brought a humanitarian appeal to his comedy. In order to express new and varied emotions subtly, he began to add his own techniques to those introduced by Sennet. Chaplin was unrivalled in mime. It was his films that first showed us how simple gestures could convey a wide range of meanings. He was incomparable also in producing different facial expressions. In the famous final close-up in *City Lights*, Chaplin holds the stalk of a rose in his hand and gives it a gentle bite; with it comes a special smile, and the look in his eyes conveys a complex mixture of hesitation and doubt. No one who has seen that close-up will ever be able to forget it. Even in our age of talkies, film-makers often ponder how to express feelings in front of a camera simply through refined and subtle acting, without resorting to words.

In a scene in the film *The Gold Rush*, Chaplin wanted to show that, driven by intense hunger, his friend was imagining him to be a chicken. In order to convey that feeling, he had to adopt a special chemical technique used in cinema. It is called 'superimposition'. As a result, we see a man one moment and a chicken the next—although the background and environment do not change. Another technique used in slapstick comedy in the silent era was called 'fast motion'. It was a trick played by the camera, but its application made human figures move and act at a far greater speed than normal, which made them look like robots, though their physical appearance remained the same.

As an artist, Buster Keaton was no less brilliant than

Chaplin, but his method was different. He appeared far more deadpan, unruffled, deep in thought. Unlike Chaplin's films, Keaton's did not offer one the chance to shed tears. His face always wore just one expression, it did not change; yet it would not be entirely wrong to call it an *absence* of expression. There is something like an abstract geometric pattern in the humorous scenes enacted by both actors—but it is more pronounced in Keaton's case. That is why Keaton's films use mid-shots and long-shots far more than close-ups.

In the interest of comedy, a certain technique that was invented became an enormously useful weapon for all comedies. It is called a tracking-shot. The camera does not remain stationary on a tripod when a tracking-shot is taken. It is placed on either a vehicle or a trolley, so that it can run alongside a moving object and capture that movement. Speed and movement form the life and soul of slapstick comedy, since it is not concerned at all with analyses of characters. Every character falls into a certain 'type'. The story does not have to be a long one; nor is there any room for slow and sentimental romantic scenes. A light-hearted story is required to move speedily, and with it move people, horses, motor cars, trains—everything. Only if the camera runs at the same speed, can a viewer's heart capture that momentum and unite with the action on the screen.

This sheer joy of moving at a fast pace—the kind of joy that can be found in classical Indian music, particularly *jalad* in *khayal*—was used by Hollywood most effectively, from the very beginning, in another type of film : the 'westerns'.

Various aspects and styles of American films influenced European directors. After the revolution in Russia, Lenin realized that cinema could be used to great advantage in the matter of propaganda. Among the young and enthusiastic directors who followed Lenin's instruction and devoted themselves to making films, three deserve special mention. They are Eisenstein, Pudovkin and Dovzhenko. What is special about them is that all three were inspired by the same ideal and, while publicizing the message of the revolution, created three successful films, each of which had a distinct and different mood.

Dovzhenko was born into a family of farmers in Ukraine. He was educated there before he went to study painting in Paris. His films have not just the beauty of paintings, but also an amazing lyrical quality. In his film *Earth*, Vassili, a farmer's son, is killed as a result of a kulak conspiracy. Other farmers arrive to carry his body away for its burial. They have to pass through an apple orchard. A close-up shows the dead Vassili's cheek being gently brushed by a ripe apple, hanging low. The feeling that single image evokes cannot be described in words— it is possible to express it only through the language of cinema.

The main subject for Pudovkin's experiments was to do with the portrayal of the innermost feelings of a person without using words. Such an idea is, of course, intrinsically related to psychology and behaviourism, and forms the basis of continued experiments by modern film-makers. A film-maker can open the door to a character's mind in front of a camera, if he can mix sharp powers of observation with an understanding of deep emotions. What is also required is the actor's own acting prowess, or—in the absence of natural talents—the ability to follow the director's instructions. Pudovkin is one of the directors who have passed this test with great success.

Among the three film-makers, Eisenstein was the most erudite thinker. He followed Griffith's system of editing and introduced his famous art of montage. Eisenstein had realized that if different shots—each of them meaningful—could be joined to one another, a whole new meaningful sentence would emerge; or even if a shot did not have a clear meaning, it could be added to either another similar shot without a distinct meaning, or one just the opposite. In each case, it would be possible to express a clear feeling or mood. This style is called 'montage'. Examples of montage may be found not just in Eisenstein's films, but in films made in any period after the arrival of talkies. Montage is an inherent part of the language of cinema.

Among other directors in Europe who made successful films in the silent era, having mastered the language of cinema, mention must be made of Carl Dreyer of Denmark; Schiller and Sjostrom of Sweden; and Murnau, Pabst, Lang and Lubitsch of Germany. The appeal of Dreyer's film *The Passion of Joan of Arc* has not faded with age. The reason is that through the use of a camera and acting, Dreyer expressed the pain and anguish in the depths of Joan's being in a way that rose much above current trends in film-making. Swedish and German film-makers have told different stories through different types of cinematic language. They were chiefly interested in relating a story; their films prove how amazingly effective photographic compositions and the use of light can be, under both natural and artificial conditions, in depicting various moods. Some of the best directors and cameramen in Germany who worked in silent films later went to Hollywood and eased the way for improvements in the talkies.

III

Most of us are aware that, soon after the talkies came, the excessive use of words turned many films almost into plays. It is the term 'talkie' that indicates why there was a misunderstanding, since sound does not imply just talking. But people realized their mistake, and the word 'talkie' was automatically replaced by 'movie' once again.

What must be remembered is that even when sound was added to silent films, it did not—and indeed it cannot—dominate the images. In other words, if images in a film are ignored and more attention is paid to sound, the language in that film is bound to be weak. Let me give an example to explain the reason. When we are deep in thought, we may well become totally unaware of sounds in our immediately vicinity. One may have to be called three times before one answers. While that may be true of our ears, it does not apply to our eyes. If our eyes are open, we can see everything even when we are preoccupied—it is just that our eyes do not remain focussed on any particular object. What it means is that between the eyes and ears, it is the former that is always more active. That is why when sound was added to images, although film directors acquired an additional tool to express their meaning, it was certainly not more powerful than images.

Nevertheless, there is no doubt that the addition of sound made the job of film-makers much simpler and, naturally, it took cinema a step closer to real life. As a result, the range of subjects films could deal with increased considerably.

It did not take long to rectify the mistakes film-makers made in the early stages of the talkies. The first talkie was made in America in 1927. A time came in the mid-1930s when it became possible to write a whole new grammar for cinematic language, bearing in mind the role played by sound. Needless to say, cinematic theorists did not overlook this job.

Some of the basic inventions made by Griffith continued to be used in the talkies. Virtually every technique used earlier in handling the camera and editing could be applied to this new language. Improvements made in equipment meant that the movement of the camera, as well as all laboratory work, were now more simplified. In fact, it was now possible to perform certain tasks that were wholly impossible before. That strengthened the language of cinema and enabled it further to express different moods and feelings.

In the silent era, it was not possible to shoot a scene either at dawn or at dusk because of an absence of suitable film; nor were there adequate filters available that might have helped a director to take a shot in bright sunlight, and pass it off as moonlight. In the mid-1930s, such tasks became easier. Colour films, one might say, created another revolution because film-makers then got the chance to convey new meanings and new thoughts through the use of colour. (It might not be irrelevant here to give an example of how colours can talk. In a black-and-white film, it is impossible to show the vermilion in a married Bengali woman's hair. In a colour film, a simple close-up of a woman's face is enough to show whether she is single or married.)

The introduction of sound brought a major change in the style of acting. In silent films, actors had to resort to using various unnatural mannerisms simply to deal with the absence of sound and words. When it became possible to speak and be heard, there was no need to use those gestures; and once the tendency to write theatrical dialogue disappeared, acting in cinema became increasingly natural. Of course, it did not mean that cinema no longer needed the element of drama. What happened was that film-makers gradually realized that drama could be created chiefly through special techniques applied by the camera and through careful editing. In order to achieve that, there was no need to pitch either the dialogue or the acting at a theatrical level.

In the mid-1930s, foreign—particularly American—films began showing an easy spontaneity, and a special quality became discernible in their application of sound. It implied that by this time many film-makers had grasped how sound must merge with image. However, this was not enough if a film were to be assessed on its aesthetic qualities. These depended on the special rhythm in a film, the creation of a special message through the joint use of sound and image, showing a deep enough understanding of the subject and characters to make them come alive and, finally, placing the stamp of the film-maker's own particular attitude and outlook on his creation.

It has been seen on several occasions that if a film is particularly rich in certain 'musical' qualities (i.e. in the matter of rhythm, tempo and contrast), those qualities can rise above the simplicity and ordinariness of the subject and reach high artistic standards. Many of John Ford's westerns, some films by Hitchcock, and some comedies made by Lubitsch fall into this category of art. At the same time, it has also been seen that whether or not a film has these 'musical' qualities, it can become a memorable work of art simply on the strength of the depth and significance of its subject and the richness of detail in the cinematic portrayal of its characters and situations. Donskoi's *Childhood of Maxim Gorky* or, in recent times, the Japanese director Yasujiro Ozu's films may be cited as examples. What they chiefly portray is what has been depicted in great literature. But they do not clash with cinematic norms because the characters and situations in these films are presented through endless minute details which are captured either by the camera or powerful acting.

It is not easy to make a synthesis of literary and musical qualities in a film since a film's structural aspects are not independent of its subject matter. In an abstract art form like music, the artist can use that form in any way he wants. That is possible also in abstract painting. What rules these forms of art is the creator's artistic spirit. But if the subject of cinema is realistic, it has a spirit of its own; so its creator cannot always do what he likes with its form especially if it has to be tied to a limited time span. Such a task becomes extremely difficult particularly when the characters in a story or the relationships between them are complex. That is why it became common practice to avoid complexities in the story of a film. Based firmly in the world of commerce, the art of cinema began taking the audience down a path that only offered tightly woven plots and simple and easy-to-understand characters.

When looking at the nature and language of films made in the 1940s, what one must consider is the responsibility of the audience as well as that of the film-makers. It was not easy for a film-maker to completely overlook what the audience would understand, what they wanted and what would please them. They wanted a story with a solid plot (be it a comedy or tragedy, a mythological story or a contemporary one), dramatic conflict, good-looking actors and actresses (hence the advent of the star system), beautiful scenery, neat and compact surroundings, and an enjoyable amalgamation of various moods, which might—at the end of the film—leave the viewers with a feeling of utter contentment.

What is remarkable is that, in spite of this rigid formula, many good films were made—although they could not possibly contain any surprises in terms of their language. It was also natural that, under those circumstances, every time a talented artist tried to do something new that fell outside all set formulae, he had to face innumerable obstacles. Even in the 1940s, a few films were made outside America which were extraordinary in terms of cinematic language. For example, one may mention the French films by Jean Vigo, *L'Atalante* or *Zero de Conduite*. However, such films were so few in number and they received such limited publicity that they failed to make a strong impact on either the general audience or the critics. Today those films are appreciated much more since times have changed, and, as a result, so has the nature of film appreciation.

IV

In 1939, the French director Jean Renoir made one of his best-known films, *La Regle du Jeu* (Rules of the Game). Film critics at the time failed to grasp that, linguistically, it was an amazing exception among films made for commercial release. One reason for this lack of a proper evaluation could be that the film was screened only for a short while. What Renoir had done in this film was expose an unpleasant but true aspect of the wealthy bourgeois class in French society. Vehement protests were made against the film and, consequently, it was removed from various cinemas. Ten years later, it was shown again to a discerning audience. That was when critics became aware of the real significance of *La Regle du Jeu*.

In order to describe a new type of story in a manner suited to cinema, Renoir was easily able to invent a new language. The first noticeable thing in *La Regle du Jeu* is that it has no single central character. The story revolves around ten or twelve wealthy and self-indulgent men and women, a few servants, and a stranger who gets mixed up with them, although he is clearly out of place in that environment. It does not have what is generally understood to be a plot; but the story moves towards a conclusion, and through the story, extraordinarily sharp and scathing comments are made against certain sections of society. Just as in Western music, where more than one melody can be played together to create a counterpoint, Renoir made a daring attempt to describe various characters and the relationships that linked one with the other, all at the same time.

The main action takes place in a country house. The entire story is spread over two or three days. There are many scenes which show two or three characters in a room in that house. At the same time, through an open door, it is possible to see another set of characters in a different room involved in a different event. Since the camera could not maintain the same distance from both sets of characters, Renoir was faced with a challenge. When shooting indoors, if objects close to *and* far from the camera must remain visible equally clearly, it is necessary to use a large number of lights. No one used to do that since it had been unanimously accepted that it was the foreground that was of primary interest, the background was secondary. Renoir was the first to use extra lights and maintain equal focus on both. Today, such a technique is well known as 'deep-focus'.

What is interesting is that Renoir went to Hollywood soon after that and made another famous film, but found no need to use deep-focus in it. Those who have seen *The Southerner* will know about the very simple language used in that film. It does not mean that Renoir had suddenly digressed as an artist. The truth is that in order to describe the simple life on a farm, Renoir did not find it necessary to re-use the complex technique used earlier in *La Regle du Jeu*.

At this point, a certain question may be asked. A great artist always leaves his mark on his creation, which is how he may be recognized through his work, regardless of its chosen subject (unless the work in question is specially commissioned, which the artist may well have undertaken against his will). The question is, can Renoir be recognized as Renoir in both the films, though they are totally different? The answer is, not if one judges the films only from the peripheries. In Renoir's case, a superficial assessment is wholly unfair since he was never one of those directors who laid the maximum emphasis only on form and structure. If one wants to get to know Renoir, one has to go deeper into his films. The most striking feature about Renoir is his humanity. His characters are not just lively; they are real people, complete with a mixture of good and bad qualities. The portrayal of human characters is as effective in *La Regle du Jeu* as it is in *The Southerner*—that is to say, Renoir used the same language in both films to speak about his fellow beings. That particular language is completely independent of fashions or trends. That is why, even twenty years later, neither film appears dated.

Three years after *La Regle du Jeu*, a new film appeared in America. It was *Citizen Kane*. Like Renoir's film, it was shot within commercial confines, but showed a huge revolutionary deviation from the established norms of film-making. In this film made by Orson Welles, the language used showed a marked rebellion against not just the traditional language that was being used in films at the time, but also certain beliefs held strongly by the American populace. The central character in *Kane* is a true American archetype. He is what is known as a tycoon: an extremely wealthy and powerful man. Usually, Americans harbour a feeling of reverence towards such characters. Orson Welles tried to expose the real nature of such a character and force the public to open its eyes to the truth. He had to create a special cinematic language to match his ruthless and analytical outlook. Until that moment, for fifteen years since the start of talkies, the crux of what virtually every director in Hollywood had accepted—consciously or unconsciously—as the gospel truth was this: the audience must not be taxed too much. In every Hollywood film that was made, careful attention was paid to the eyes, ears and minds of the viewers. Welles struck a blow at all three at once, without displaying the slightest qualm. Visually, *Kane* showed a harsh sharpness which permeated every scene (incidentally, the cameraman Gregg Toland used deep-focus in this film). Traditionally, every make-up man and cameraman in Hollywood had to keep a careful eye on the appearance of the heroine, in case blemishes on her skin became obvious. Welles refused to follow this practice in the case of his own heroine.

Aurally, for the first time, dialogue in a film was presented in a highly realistic and unmitigated form; and mentally, the audience was totally taken aback by a new style of flashback that—though justified—was most complex in nature.

Citizen Kane has been universally acknowledged as an epoch-making creation in the history of cinema. Orson Welles made *The Magnificent Ambersons* after *Kane* and continued with linguistic experiments. There is a lot to learn in these films regarding the special and varied use of lenses, light and camera angles in dramatic sequences. However, both films were much in advance of their time and the audience found them ultra-modern. Consequently, both failed commercially, and a disappointed Welles was soon forced to turn to making thrillers. His later films bear plenty of evidence of his originality in terms of style and structure, but the seriousness and social consciousness shown in the choice of subject in *Kane* and *Ambersons* is not discernible in these later films.

The Japanese director Akira Kurosawa's film *Rashomon* was screened in the Venice Film Festival in 1951. It made an amazing impact on all critics and connoisseurs who were present. The reason was the totally new subject that *Rashomon* dealt with as well as the extraordinary language used in the film. The East met the West in this film in a striking manner. Japanese kabuki, the method adopted in acting in the noh dance-dramas in Japan, and the art and composition of Japanese woodcuts fitted in, with surprising ease, with the speed normally witnessed in American westerns, retaining—at the same time—the detailed, leisurely character analyses that is the hallmark of great novels in any country.

The later films of Kurosawa show that he was able to change the language in his films any way he liked, in the interest of his subject. What is most remarkable is that although he uses various styles, he manages to avoid a great hotchpotch.

Another Japanese director deserves special mention here for his very original use of film language. He is Yasujiro Ozu. It seems from his films that either he has never seen a single film made in the West, or he has no notion of the grammar of the language used there. Ozu does, of course, divide a scene into different shots, but apart from that, does not appear to have any faith in any other technique.

In his films, the camera remains stationary. Only rarely can one see the use of a tracking shot; and even when one does, it is clear that it is not used for conventional reasons. The ideas we may have formed regarding the variety created by the use of speed and rhythm in films from different countries are totally absent in Ozu's films. There may be a difference in the distance between the camera and each object, but the lens of his camera is placed, in every shot, at the same height where a person's eyes would be if he were kneeling on the floor in the Japanese style. The overall visual impact in Ozu's films therefore acquires an unyielding purity, which the general audience may well find tiresome. Yet it would be wrong to say that his films do not make successful cinema because, to start with, the acting in his films is always amazingly natural and expressive. Secondly, his characters can always be recognized as real people of flesh and blood, and each character comes alive through various realistic details. A uniform expression of emotions and moods, and a mild conflict between numerous characters in Ozu's films create a kind of inward momentum. Such momentum can be felt only in one's heart; and it is only Ozu's films which prove that even an inward momentum can make a film throb with life.

V

Ten years ago, the young French director, Francois Truffaut, used a freeze for the first time in the last shot of the last scene in his film, *400 Blows*. I do not know if a freeze was used in any film before *400 Blows*, but it may be said without any doubt that, even if it was, it did nothing to attract the attention of film enthusiasts. Before he became a film-maker, Truffaut belonged to a group of critics who wrote for the famous French film journal, *Cahiers du Cinema*. Having seen films, both good and bad, from different countries, and having come into contact with one of the best-known critics in the world—Andre Bazin— the foundation on which Truffaut was able to stand became rock solid. Other film-makers such as Godard, Chabrol and Rivette also learnt film-making in the same atmosphere as Truffaut. It was they who led the New Wave movement.

In the language used in *400 Blows* there is a beautiful easy spontaneity. The first part of the film may remind one of other famous French directors—for instance, Renoir, Claire or Becker. It is the second half that reveals the film's special qualities. What Truffaut has done here is draw on not only the techniques already used in cinema, but also some of those practised on television. The central character is a delinquent boy. Unable to cope with his behaviour, his parents put him in a correctional institute. There is a scene where the boy is shown being questioned. It is obvious that Truffaut does not use dialogue that the boy could have memorized from the script. The questions were made up and thrown at him on the spot as he faced the camera, and he answered them instinctively as best as he could. As a result, the particular expressions that appear on his face would have been virtually impossible to capture if traditional cinematic practices were adopted to shoot the scene. The lines spoken by the boy are not directly related to the main story, nor are they required to be thus related. If the dialogue in a film is supposed to explain the story, it ought to be written beforehand, or there would be problems. But in this scene created by Truffaut, the boy speaking his lines, using his own words spontaneously helps in achieving, in a highly successful and novel manner, a major goal of all dialogue in a film: making a character come alive.

The last scene of *400 Blows* shows the boy running away from the correctional institute. He runs through the village towards the sea. He has heard that the sea is not far from his school and, if he can reach it, he thinks all his problems would come to an end.

The entire scene, which runs to about four minutes, was taken in one single tracking shot. It changes when the boy gets close to the sea. Then the camera 'pans' (i.e. its handle is turned to make it change direction) with the boy to the area where the waves are crashing against the shore. Then it stops. The boy cannot run any further, the road has ended. He must turn back. After a few seconds, he wheels around and appears to run straight back in the direction of the viewers, i.e. he runs back at the camera. Even as he is running, the shot suddenly

freezes and becomes a still. That is where the film ends, with
the boy caught in mid-run, facing the audience.

It is easy enough to see that the use of a freeze here is not
just startling, but also deeply meaningful. In fact, it might be
called a stroke of genius. The boy has nowhere to go. So, no
matter how fast he runs, it will be no different from standing
still. His desire to run away, and the director's wish to say, 'there's
no point in running' have both been expressed through that
shot. There is a message even in the way the boy looks at the
viewers. It seems as if he is trying to say, 'You, the entire society,
are responsible for my situation. *You* go and figure out what
is to become of boys like me.'

Freeze shots are now being used in many films, though the
purpose behind their use in each case is difficult to fathom.
One may explain the problem by drawing an analogy with a
person's smile. It makes sense if someone smiles because there
is a clear reason to do so. If, however, a person smiles just
because he—or she—looks nice when smiling, it then becomes
an affectation, its only aim is to seek attention; and if someone
smiles without any apparent reason, it is natural to see that
as a sign of mental disorder. Even if such a smile has a meaning,
it is known only to the person smiling. Therefore it is both
personal and secret, and there is no question of others responding
to that smile.

The use of a freeze shot need not necessarily be dramatic.
When a moment becomes special to us and makes an
impression, we often say, 'It is worth framing!' That is merely
a figure of speech; but the language of cinema can give it a
finite shape through the use of a freeze. Those who have seen
Truffaut's *Jules et Jim* will have noticed that a freeze was used
more than once in that film. A little smile, a brief glance, a
rhythmic and expressive physical gesture—Truffaut has frozen

many of these things and framed them for a second. But the freezes used in *Jules et Jim* are very different from the one shown in *400 Blows*. It is also worth noting that in his later films which have different themes and different moods, Truffaut abandoned the use of freeze almost completely. (The very traditional language of *La Peau Douce* is particularly noteworthy.) As a matter of fact, the language of *Jules et Jim* is naturally linked to its subject, and so both are unusual. The central figure in this film—a woman called Catherine—controls the movement and style of the entire film. Catherine is fiercely independent and reckless. She does not care about social norms, and is quite unconventional. If it was Truffaut's intention to criticize such a character, he would have told his story in a traditionally dramatic manner. But he fell in love with the character of Catherine, and identified with her completely as he made the film. Consequently, as the story proceeded, her character made an impact on the narrative style, time and again. In the later films of Truffaut, however, such techniques in language have been absent, which made many viewers bemoan the fact that he has lost his originality. It is my belief that because Truffaut is a great artist, he does not go in for linguistic gimmicks independent of his subject. In each of his films, it is possible to see a remarkable harmony between his subject and narrative style.

In the matter of creating a revolution in the language of cinema, Jean-Luc Godard was a pioneer. Before discussing his works, we must remind ourselves of one thing. Over the last fifteen or twenty years, a difference in attitude has become evident in Western art, literature and music. Traditional values have been widely affected for various socio-political reasons. A lack of faith in the existing social system and a cynicism about established moral values are emerging through different levels in art and literature. Naturally, this is influencing cinema, both in its subject and style. Subjects that were considered improper even ten years ago are not seen as such any more. In the matter of techniques, attempts are being made to remove softness and gentleness from films. Techniques applied to make-up, acting, placement of lights for the camera, dialogue, editing—everything is trying to fit in with the new attitudes in this new age. Even the use of background music is now on the wane. Earlier, nearly 75 per cent of every Hollywood film was submerged in background music. Today, this easy way to convey or highlight a mood, which was external to a film's subject matter, is being abandoned in favour of only real sounds from real life. Plenty of people are trying hard to prove that cinema is not a medium meant just for entertainment, it is serious art. The viewers, at first taken aback and confused by such attempts, are now getting used to these new attitudes.

A few films had given us an idea of this new way of thinking long before the appearance of Godard or New Wave films. In the neo-realist era of Italian films, directors like De Sica, Rossellini, De Santis and others took new actors and brought them out of the studio, without any make-up, to shoot their films on the streets in a realistic environment. A new social awareness, combined with that environment, gave cinema a new look. However, no film from this era could step out of established norms in terms of either language or structure. In films like *Bicycle Thieves* or *Open City*, if the outer layer of realism is peeled off, the framework that is exposed is really not very different from the framework of ancient Greek drama. Some years after neo-realism came into existence, this new mood and new stance became clearer in films made in the early 1950s. In this connection, mention may be made of Antonioni's

Il Grido, Bunuel's *Nazarin* and Bresson's *Diary of a Country Priest*.

Like Truffaut, Godard was among the panel of critics who wrote for *Cahiers du Cinema*. He was familiar with films of all types, from all ages. In his reviews, almost from the beginning, he showed a feeling of contempt for convention. The other thing that came through was his erudition, social consciousness and leftist leanings.

Godard began his film-making with some short films. I have seen one of them (*Every Young Man Is Called Patrick*). It is clear that he made the film only to gain experience. Godard handles his job with expertise, and the film bears traces of modern thinking—but, all things considered, there is no sign of rebelliousness. The first long feature film made by Godard is the highly acclaimed *Breathless*. It is from this film that he began breaking convention.

If one is to understand the language used in *Breathless*, one must remember one thing: Godard's chief aim was to make a film on a low budget. He knew very well that making a commercial film meant obeying certain rules that have nothing to do with art. Godard was not prepared to be governed by such rules. Yet it was clear that if his films ran constantly at a loss, he would soon have to stop making films altogether. So he discovered various ways to limit expenses. There are certain things one has got to do—such as hire a camera or a laboratory, which offer virtually no scope to cut down costs. Using a great deal of raw stock in a film will raise expenses which can be reduced if one stops worrying about a certain type of technical perfection. Also, if the actors are experienced, shots may be taken without using up too much film since the need to take the same shot more than once—just to correct lapses in acting—

is likely to be less. Godard, therefore, did not even think of using new and inexperienced actors. The hero and heroine of *Breathless* are both professional actors.

Then there is all the cumbersome equipment that is required without which it is not possible to achieve technical lustre in a film. A tracking shot, for instance, is taken by placing the camera on a trolley, which runs along a track on the floor. This is most time consuming, and a lot has to be done to ensure that the trolley runs smoothly on the track. At the same time, it has to be remembered that, when shooting a film, time is money. So Godard did not bother with a trolley at all. He simply handed a camera to the cameraman and asked him to walk as he took a tracking shot. As a result, the cameraman's hand trembled, and that tremble spread through the shot taken, creating an unclear and hazy effect. But Godard remained undaunted. He continued to take further shots in the same manner, one after the other. In the end, that tremble in every shot became a part of Godard's style, as if he wanted to say— a film is not a lifeless, flawless object made by a machine; it is made by man, so there is nothing wrong if it carries evidence of the work a man has done with his own hands, and that should not stand in the way of a just artistic evaluation.

Techniques such as 'dissolve' and 'fade' are handled through a chemical process, hence they too are expensive. Godard dropped those two from his film almost completely, and used cuts to go from one scene to another. If a novel is not divided into chapters, and there is a long, uninterrupted description of events, the average reader is bound to stumble, even if the events are discrete and not related to one another. The use of jump-cuts in Godard's film caused much agitation at first among his viewers. Gradually, even these jump-cuts became a part of his own cinematic language.

The language he finally created by saving costs wherever he could fitted in beautifully with the unconventional story of *Breathless*. It *is* a love story, but those who have seen it will know how different it is from a traditional love story with a happy ending.

The modern thoughts and attitudes evident in Godard's first film became clearer and more uncompromising in his later films. Even so, from time to time, Godard brought modern poetry to his work, brought compassion and—accordingly—his language changed a little and became more simple, for instance in a film like *Pierrot le Fou* or *Masculin Feminin*. Most of his films, however, bear a mood that is both harsh and ultra-modern, be it in its subject or narrative style. That style contains elements not just from literature, music, painting or drama, but also shows the influence of television, press reports, language used in advertisement, in essays, and even pop art. In spite of this hotchpotch, Godard's films are artistically successful chiefly for two reasons. First, he has a remarkably clear understanding of today's reality. Second, he also has an extraordinary ability to effect a synthesis of apparently contradictory cinematic language. Such a thing is impossible to achieve unless one has a firm grasp of the language used. It is also worth noting that although Godard uses different language to say different things about the same subject in the same film, it is always clear that that is evidence of his erudition and wit—not an aberration of his mind.

It is not easy to understand Godard's films. But that is not Godard's fault. It is the fault of the mentality that has taken cinema down the path of least resistance simply by threatening film-makers with the possibility of financial loss, and forced their audience to tread the same path with them.

Like Godard, many directors abroad are making films on

the problems of modern life. Unfortunately, virtually each one of them is blindly copying Godard's style. They do not have his intellect, or wit, or, indeed, a thorough knowledge of cinematic convention. The last is important simply because if, in the matter of art, rules have to be broken, it is necessary to have a clear idea of what those rules are, and what new rules may be applied to replace old ones. Godard's imitators do not seem to have any such idea.

Of course, there are still some film-makers working in foreign countries who have made successful films that reflect their times and age. They achieved this without using Godard's ultra-modern style and outlook. No film critic or connoisseur of cinema has, as yet, used the word 'old-fashioned' for these film-makers. In this regard, mention must be made of European directors like Bergman, Antonioni, Bellocchio, Olmi, Pasolini, Bunuel, Forman and Jancso, as well as Japanese film-makers like Teshigahara and Ichikawa. It is not as if they have all discarded well-structured plots or the elements of drama from their films; nor have they all become difficult to understand. The 'modernity' in their films is not visible externally. In most cases, it lies merely in a particular outlook which is expressed through a certain style. That is not surprising, since it is not mandatory for every film-maker to harbour the same rebellious attitude as Godard, and rebellion alone does not define modernity. It would be extremely regrettable if a powerful medium like cinema, with so much potential, suddenly began to speak in the same style and same tone.

As long as an artist can enjoy his individual freedom, and as long as the same subject and environment can create a different resonance in the minds of different perceptive and sensitive artists, the same artists are bound to express themselves at any given time through different modes and appear in different garbs.

4

Soviet Cinema

Before one starts talking about the evolution of Soviet cinema, it is necessary to say a few things about cinema in Russia before the Revolution.

Towards the end of the nineteenth century, motion pictures were born at about the same time in America, France and England. Those moving images created enormous wonder and excitement in the mind of the general public. Consequently, people involved in the discovery of moving pictures were left in no doubt about its future as a business. So, in order to publicize the glory of their golden discovery, they began showing in various countries what they had created.

The same year in which Nicholas II had his coronation— in 1896—the Lumiere Company of France arranged the first cinematographic exhibition in Moscow. A short time later, motion pictures made by Robert Paul of England and Thomas Edison of USA were shown in Russia. As a result, the Russian public, as well as Nicholas himself, became totally enchanted with the medium.

Among the early viewers of cinema were a few Russian scholars. Vladimir Stassof was, at the time, the best-known music critic. Edison's film of a running train reminded him

---

'Soviet Biplab', *Parichay*, Puja Issue, 1967.

of *Anna Karenina*. Maxim Gorky's comments are particularly noteworthy with regard to that ancient cinema. He said, 'People today do not find much excitement in the ordinary events of their daily lives. But the same ordinary events acquire a deep dramatic form in cinema and stir the hearts of the same people. I fear that perhaps, one day, the world portrayed in films will overtake the real world and occupy the mind and heart of every human being.'

At that time, there were close economic and political links between France and Russia. So, French film companies such as Geaumont and Pathe quickly captured the Russian market. Most of their films were related to events in real life, i.e. what is now known as newsreel. Gradually, films began to turn to novels and drama on which to base their stories, and the popularity of cinema increased considerably.

In 1903, Guttsmann became the first Russian distributor to join the business of distributing French films in Russia. Encouraged by his success, many other Russian businessmen became involved with film distribution.

Over the next three years, cinema continued to thrive as a commercial venture, in spite of the war between Russia and Japan, political instability, unrest and revolt among workers. In 1907, Alexander Drankoff became the first Russian producer. The following year, the first Russian film produced by Drankoff—*Stenka Razin*—was screened. It made a lot of money. For a long time, the Russian market was led by Drankoff and his rival, Khanjonkoff. Drankoff's most memorable achievement was getting Tolstoy to face the camera. Tolstoy was known to object to being photographed, so it came as no surprise when, initially, he objected to cinematography. However, when he saw samples of what the moving image could do, he became most enthusiastic. It was his view that Russian film-makers should avoid fictitious stories and aim to show the real lives of Russian peasants in their films.

The First World War did not do any damage to Russian cinema commercially; on the contrary, by putting a stop to the import of European films, it boosted the production of indigenous Russian films. Among those who made a significant contribution to the evolution of Russian cinema, in addition to Drankoff and Khanjonkoff, from the first Russian film in 1907 to just before the start of the Revolution, were the joint producers Thieman and Reinhart; directors like Goncharov, Protazanov and Yevgeny Bouye; writer and dramatist, Leonid Andreiev; the producer of plays, Meyerhold; and the revolutionary poet, Mayakovski.

Andreiev's name must be mentioned, before anyone else's, when talking about Russian writers and artists who were prepared to give cinema the status of art, and who employed themselves in the business of film-making towards that end. In France, Italy and Germany, leading writers like Apollinaire and d'Annunzio and Gerhart Hauptmann did not hesitate to play a role in the making of films. Andreiev wanted other Russian writers to discard their snobbery and come forward to help Russian cinema. He pulled what strings he could, as a result of which more than one writer entered into contracts with film producers to work as scriptwriters. However, undesirable interference from the producers meant that none of their scripts could reach the screen in their original undistorted form.

In 1913, Mayakovski's first brush with cinema ended most tragically. The producer, Parsky, heard the screenplay Mayakovski had written, and rejected it outright. Yet, only a short time later, Mayakovski saw a film produced by the same Parsky, which had used a screenplay that was almost completely identical to the one written by Mayakovski.

Meyerhold, one of the pioneers in modern stagecraft, made a film in 1914 from Oscar Wilde's *Picture of Dorian Gray*. Those who have seen it are of the view that it was something so new that what it achieved in the history of silent films may be compared with Germany's *Caligari*.

Sadly, one of the brightest stars of the Russian theatre, Konstantin Stanislavsky, harboured a lot of negative feelings about cinema until the end of his days.

II

During his exile in Zurich, after a day's work, Lenin frequently spent his evenings in cinemas. It was not merely to relax and to look for entertainment. Lenin's chief aim was to watch the newsreels of different countries and observe the behaviour of both the people of those countries and their leaders. That cinema can help expand one's knowledge to an amazing degree was something Lenin learnt while he was in Zurich.

When the First World War started, at first a strong wave of patriotism swept through the whole of Russia. That feeling was also reflected in Russian cinema. May Russia prosper and may Germany be destroyed—that was the message in films made in Russia in the first year of the war. But in the second year, anarchy spread everywhere and German and Austrian armies reclaimed their lost territories, which made events take a different turn. Even then the Russian public remained disinterested in the war and a deep distrust regarding the reign of the Czar began gripping their minds. Russian cinema did not fail to capture that mood and show how the old establishment was crumbling.

Though Jay Leyda says, 'Not normal men and women, but devils, ascetics, vampires people the films of the Russian winter of 1916,' there was still no question of the film industry suffering a financial loss. There were 164 companies employed in the business of production and distribution at the time, with a total capital of four million roubles. What Russian cinema lacked was not money, but order and reassurance regarding its future.

As a result of the revolution in February 1917, the workers in the film industry began to feel a little hopeful, but the provisional government dashed those hopes, at least temporarily. It would be irrelevant here to describe in detail the movement and final conclusion of this particular chapter of Russian history, from February to October 1917; but it is important to remember that a month before October, an important meeting of the workers was held, at which some decisions were made about the nature and aims of art in a socialist society. Naturally, one of the subjects discussed at this meeting was cinema. The post-Revolution Proletarian Cultural Association (Proletkult) was formed at this meeting.

When victory for the Bolsheviks seemed inevitable during the Revolution, many ballet and cinema artists became concerned about their future and moved to southern Russia, outside the area occupied by the Bolsheviks. Later, they had to leave Russia altogether and move to the West, i.e. to Europe and America. Among those who fled Russia few were ordinary workers—most were film producers, directors and actors. Not many returned to their country; but there are very few examples of such Russians achieving success and carving a permanent niche for themselves in foreign lands.

Eventually, in August 1919, the film industry in Soviet Russia was nationalized. Between October 1917 and August 1919, a few noteworthy events took place. First, the first cinema committee was born, controlled by the state. Second, a films subcommittee was established, headed by Kruppskaya, which came under the education department. Businessmen in the film industry did not like being under the scrutiny of the government. So some more producers escaped to the south, together with their film-making equipment. Naturally, that led to something close to a crisis. In the end, the government was forced to pass a law to stop more people from running away. They also formed another new committee to encourage the remaining producers to make films. In the beginning, the posters issued by the cinema committee laid more emphasis on education than art in cinema. It was the director who was left to worry about art in a film.

In March 1918, Mayakovski found the opportunity he had been deprived of before. He wrote four screenplays—in quick succession—for Neptune Company of Moscow. Not only that, he even acted as the central character in one of them (a film version of Jack London's *Martin Eden*). But, according to Mayakovski himself, not one of those four screenplays resulted in good films as the direction in each was faulty.

On 1 May 1918, the cinema committee appointed a young cinematographer to film the first May Day celebration in Red Square in Moscow. His name was Eduard Tisse. In later years, he gained much international acclaim as Eisenstein's cameraman.

The same year, on 27 June, the first Soviet feature film, *The Signal*, was shown. The director was Alexander Arkatov. Shortly afterwards, the Agit-train came into being. This train carried provision for printing newspapers and handbills; crew and equipment to make films, as well as groups of people to write and enact new plays. The final destination of the train was the eastern border of Russia. The Red Army was then fighting the Czech army to reclaim Kazan. The Agit-train was created to encourage and inspire the Red Army. Eduard Tisse was among those who led the film-making crew. A young poet, the twenty-year-old Dziga Vertov, came forward to help with editing whatever was filmed.

Having seen the major efforts made by the Soviet government in order to spread education, Maxim Gorky felt moved enough to come forward himself and make a few suggestions, through a lecture, regarding cinema and drama. What he said in that lecture focussed on how the history of human civilization could be presented to the general public through these two powerful media. Unfortunately, in terms of equipment, manpower and capital, Soviet cinema had not yet reached a stage where it might have been possible to take Gorky's noble plans to successful fruition. Twenty-five screenplays planned and envisaged by Gorky, therefore, remained only on paper.

III

Soon after the nationalization of Soviet cinema, an American film was released in Russia, which made a deep impression on both the public and those from the film world. That film was Griffith's *Intolerance*. Later, other films by Griffith were also shown all over Russia. Even Eisenstein openly recognized Griffith's influence on Russian cinema.

In 1918, Eisenstein finished studying civil engineering in Petrograd and joined the Red Army. He made some drawings at that time to be used on the Agit-train as material for propaganda. He returned to the engineering school after the war, but left it soon afterwards to join the Proletkult, and got involved with Russian art.

In the meantime, a state-owned film school had started. Among the teachers there was one of the cameramen on the Agit-train, Lev Kuleshov. He had been a part of the film industry in pre-Revolution Russia.

During the first May Day celebrations held at that film school, another man came into the limelight who was to become one of the best-known names in Russian cinema. He was Vsevolod Pudovkin, a chemist. Inspired by Griffith's *Intolerance*, he came forward to work in films, and began his career as an actor.

Various others followed the three men mentioned above and worked together to build and strengthen cinema in Soviet Russia. Among them were Alexander Dovzhenko, Gregori Kozintsev, Leonid Trauburg, Sergei Yutkevitch, Mikhail Chiaureli, Friedrich Ermler, Sergei Vasiliev and Mikhail Kalatozov. In the years that followed the Revolution, Russians naturally had to face economic hardships. Commercial ties with Europe had snapped, resulting in acute shortages in film equipment and raw stock. In order to solve that problem, Lenin introduced a New Economic Policy (NEP), which made commercial transactions a little easier. However, Russia was soon hit by a nationwide famine. Film producers made films on the effects of that famine and arranged to show them everywhere in the country, with a view to raising funds to deal with it. Three such films were made in quick succession. Pudovkin wrote the script for one of them. Another film, called *The Famine in Russia*, was made by the Norwegian traveller, Dr Fritzof Nansen. His film was shown in England, France and America, and was thus able to evoke widespread sympathy for the situation in Russia.

After that, in various states of Russia, autonomous film departments were established. Studios in Georgia and Ukraine saw fresh activity as new films began to be made. Kuleshov started new experiments in film-making in the state film school. Pudovkin joined Kuleshov at about the same time.

Lenin had declared that in the newly formed USSR, films rooted in the real world were of far greater value than those that took their stories from fiction. In order to spread the socialist ideology and produce an authentic picture of life in Soviet Russia, *Kino-Pravda* came into being in May 1922. It was a film version of a weekly newspaper. Dziga Vertov, who worked on the Agit-train, supervised the filming of *Kino-Pravda*. In fact, *Kino-Pravda* may be seen as the father of the modern weekly newsreel.

At about the same time, various film magazines appeared in Russia. *Kino*, *Photo-Kino*, and some others appeared almost simultaneously. *Kino-Gazetta*, a weekly magazine which was first published in September 1923, is still in existence.

On behalf of the Proletkult, Eisenstein arranged Ostrovski's play, *Enough Simplicity in Every Wise Man*, to be performed. He had to film a satirical piece called *Glumov's Film Diary* as a part of that play. That was Eisenstein's maiden venture as a film-maker.

On 17 August 1923, a notice was issued by the Soviet government to the effect that all private film enterprises were being abolished, and the government would henceforth take full responsibility for production and distribution of all films. It was after this that the golden era in silent Russian films began. In an amazingly short time, Russian films became well known throughout the world. Among the films that were largely responsible for this were a satirical film called *The Extraordinary Adventures of Mr West in the Land of the Bolsheviks* made by

Kuleshov, two films by Pudovkin called *Death Ray* and *Mechanics of the Brain*, Vertov's *Kino-Eye* which was a collection of stories based on real events, and Eisenstein's *Strike*.

Kuleshov made *Mr West* chiefly to test some of his original theories regarding acting in films. The style of acting adopted in films made in Russia before the Revolution followed the same style used on the stage. What was done in Moscow Art Theatre was considered sacrosanct even in cinema. Kuleshov was of the view that acting in films ought to be completely different and have a distinct nature of its own. So he put his belief into practice, made his actors perform with a totally new style and achieved complete success.

In his first film, *Death Ray*, Pudovkin too initiated a few new ideas. He was the first to prove that in order to depict crowd sequences with any authenticity it was necessary that the 'crowd' be made to act. Further, he did away with the practice of getting actors to portray workers and, in filming the scenes involving the workers' revolution, got real workers to act instead.

With *Kino-Eye*, Dziga Vertov proved that if the camera places itself face-to-face with reality and, embellished with thoughtful detailing, reflects that reality, films need not depend on fiction to win favour with the audience. It may be noted here that the principles underlying the current cinéma-vérité is not very different from those articulated forty years ago in *Kino-Eye*. It is pertinent to consider what Vertov had to say: 'It is necessary to get out of this limited circle of ordinary vision—reality must be recorded not by imitating it, but by broadening the range ordinarily encompassed by the human eye.'

Eisenstein revolutionized Soviet cinema with *Strike*. In those days, the absence of a conventional plot or story and the lack of a 'hero' central to the narrative were unheard of. The film deals with the mechanics of a pre-Revolution workers' strike—how it originates and how the owners use force to break it up. With the help of well-selected character types, backdrops and detailing, and thanks to creative editing and screenplay, Eisenstein managed to infuse *Strike* with a dramatic vigour. Eisenstein termed the style of editing he evolved the 'montage of attractions'. According to him, every shot in the film should be imbued with a certain quality which, when the shot is seen in isolation and in totality with the shots preceding and following it, would progressively attract, startle and agitate the viewer.

By 1925, the twentieth anniversary of the revolution of 1905, Eisenstein had left the Proletkult to join a studio in Moscow as a director. He was requested to make a film of the events pertaining to the revolution and given a screenplay based on incidents culled from the revolution. This screenplay ultimately became *Potemkin*. An analysis of this renowned and multilayered film is not necessary here. It must however be mentioned that though the film was greeted with enthusiasm by Soviet critics, it took Eisenstein some time to release the film. It was only after the frenzied praise the film garnered in Berlin, 1925, that the film was widely screened in Russia.

The next worthwhile Soviet film centred around the same revolution was Pudovkin's *Mother*, based on the novel by Gorky. Like *Potemkin*, *Mother* too is an unforgettable part of Soviet cinema history. A comparison of the two films reveals a subtle difference in the perspectives of their great directors. Eisenstein's structure displayed a clear preference for geometric precision. If in the process the human element of the material was affected, the basic material remains simple, strong and supple. In Pudovkin's film, it is the humanism and lyricism which stand out. The structure is important no doubt, but the mathematical precision of Eisenstein is absent. To give an example from the world of music, if Eisenstein reminds one of Bach, Pudovkin approximates Beethoven.

The third stalwart of silent Soviet cinema, Alexander Dovzhenko, comes into the picture in 1925. Dovzhenko was an artist. Discerning that in a socialist society a film-maker would have better prospects than an artist, Dovzhenko left his home in Kharkov to come to Odessa's film studio. Within a short span, he gathered relevant experience in films by making two comedies, before proceeding to make the allegorical *Zvenigora*. When the film was complete, the manager at Odessa's film studio sent it to their representative at Moscow. Bewildered with the film, the said representative arranged for the film to be shown to Eisenstein and Pudovkin. Eisenstein said, 'Pudovkin and I had a wonderful task; to answer the questioning eyes of the auditorium with a joyful welcome of our new colleague and to be the first to greet him!'

Over the next four years, a number of films helped Soviet cinema gain a lot of respect all over the world. These included Eisenstein's *The General Line* and *October*, Pudovkin's *The End of St. Petersberg* and *Storm over Asia*, Dovzhenko's *Arsenal* and *Earth*, Turin's documentary *Turksir*, Room's *Bed and Sofa*, Ermler's *Fragments of an Empire*, and Mikhail Rom's *The Ghost That Will Not Return*.

During the editing of *The General Line*, Eisenstein took up a teaching assignment with the State Institute. He wanted to disseminate among young students the fundamental principles of cinema which he had formulated from his exhaustive study of film and film material.

After a year as a teacher at the State Institute, Eisenstein travelled to America with his cameraman Tisse and compatriot Alexandrov. The talkies had started in America in 1927. The primary goal behind this trip was to find out facts about this new development. Eisenstein was also conceptualizing a film based on Marx's *Das Kapital*, and he believed that this was not possible without a direct contact with capitalist America.

In America, Eisenstein was approached by a couple of companies in Hollywood to make films. Nothing, however, came out of it. Eventually, urged by Upton Sinclair, he went to Mexico to shoot *Que Viva Mexico*, a chronological account of the progress of Mexican civilization. For two years he worked tirelessly, shooting thousands and thousands of feet of film, before returning to Russia, keeping the negatives with Sinclair. It was agreed that once the negatives were developed, Sinclair would ship the same to Russia for editing. However, a few days later, Sinclair wrote to Eisenstein that to recover his laboratory costs, he had sold the entire footage to a company in Hollywood.

In the meantime, talkies had begun to be shot in Russia, and the first Soviet talkie, Nicolai Ekk's *Road to Life*, had already been screened. Film magazines carried extensive writings on the relationship between image and sound. One after the other, Pudovkin (*Deserter*), Dovzhenko (*Ivan*), Yutkevich (*Golden Mountains*), and Kuleshov (*Men and Jobs*), made talking films. Given that the talkies came a little later in Russia than in other countries, the early Soviet talkies did not have the flaws that early American and European talkies had—excessive dialogues and staginess.

Despite having made four remarkable films in the silent era, Eisenstein did not find due recognition with the authorities on his return from America. By this time, a certain measure of government censorship had been imposed on artists. The story that Eisenstein had decided upon for his next film was rejected by his superior Shumyatski, who instructed him to make a film on another subject. That did not work out either, and Eisenstein decided to give up film-making to concentrate on teaching, a vocation he was no less enthusiastic about. In a short time, he revolutionized the ways of teaching at the university.

IV

Over the last thirty-five years, ever since the advent of the talkies in Soviet cinema, government interference has made it difficult for many a frontline Russian film-maker to make the kind of film he would have liked to. In many cases, film-makers have had to make suitable changes to their works as per government directives. While at times films have been banned, the performances of a large number of films have been adversely affected thanks to severe governmental criticism. This is primarily why over the last thirty years film lovers worldwide have been hard pressed to remember the names of even thirty films coming out of the Soviet Union, a nation which produces on an average a hundred films a year, a nation whose silent films have been acclaimed as classics of international cinema.

One reason for this is obviously the fact that there are in the matter of film production certain inherent dualities which are independent of the society in which the films are screened. It is, for example, impossible to make films independent of audience expectations—this is true as much of America as it is of Soviet Russia. At the same time, this audience expectation is not quantifiable. How then does an artist reconcile his art with audience expectation? Secondly, while in a capitalist society the director's artistic freedom is impinged upon by the producer or the studio owners, in a socialist society it is the government which lays down the rules within which the film-maker will have to operate. Every major Russian film-maker—Eisenstein,

Pudovkin, Dovzhenko—have had to bear the cross of governmental interference at some time or the other in their careers. And it does not have to be reiterated that these are all talented, socially conscious film-makers.

Some Soviet films of 1930s are still incandescent in their brilliance. These include Eisenstein's *Alexander Nevsky*, *Chapayev* by the Vasiliev brothers, Vertov's *Three Songs of Lenin*, Donskoi's *The Gorky Trilogy*, and Dovzhenko's *Earth*. With the onset of the Second World War, a wave of patriotic fervour brought about a meeting of the minds between the government and film-makers, much like what was witnessed at the time of the First World War. As a result, a few memorable anti-fascism films and some astounding documentaries saw the light of day. Among other war-time films, Pudovkin's *General Suvorov* and Dovzhenko's biography of the famous Russian horticulturist Michurin are worth mentioning. But, in the absence of artistic freedom, none of these attained the status of a classic.

Eisenstein's *Ivan the Terrible* too was made during the Second World War. Conceptualized as a mammoth three-part film, its first part was released in 1944. The second part was banned during the reign of Stalin on the grounds that the director had distorted history in his depiction of Ivan's cruelty, and in the process had displayed reactionary tendencies. Fortunately, seeing the second part of the film in the post-Stalin era, we realized that if there is one work of film which can be placed in the league of Shakespeare's literary output, it is Eisenstein's two-part, incomplete biography of Ivan. Over the years arguments have raged, and still continue to do so, over if at all this is a film, or whether the director, in placing the work in an operatic framework has belittled the art of film-making, or whether a film-maker has the right to distort history.

Thankfully, great works of art are way beyond the reach of critics.

Though state censorship of films has eased in the post-Stalin era, contemporary Soviet cinema is rather lacklustre. Its depiction of modern life, in particular interpersonal relationships in present-day society, is simplistic to say the least. Once in a while, however, one does come across first-class work, particularly in the genre of historicals and biographies, and in period films based on the works of Shakespeare, Chekov, Tolstoy, and other such literary giants. When it comes to variety in acting skills, luminous art direction, innovative costumes and screenplay, subtlety in the use of colour and music, and in social graces, Soviet cinema continues to be as unparalleled today as it was in its heyday.

Thus, if Vasili's dance sequence in the open fields on a moonlit night in *Earth* or the nightmarish Odessa steps massacre sequence in *Potemkin* remain unforgettable, Cherkassov's portrayal of Ivan, Smoktunovsky's depiction of Hamlet, and Bondarchuk's *Othello* are equally memorable. If Prokofiev's music in *Nevsky* and *Ivan* haunts one even now, so does Dovzhenko's use of colour in *Michurin*, *Hamlet*'s Fort Elsinore, and Natasha's dance in *War and Peace*.

5

Bengali Films in the Past

I happened to see my first Bengali film the day I went to see Johnny Weissmuller's *Tarzan the Ape Man* and couldn't get a ticket. *Tarzan* was being screened at 'The Globe'. It was the first show of the first Tarzan film since the beginning of talkies. Close to 'The Globe' was 'The Albion' (the modern 'Regal') which was showing *Kaal Parinay*. An uncle had taken me to see *Tarzan*. I hardly got the chance to see more than a couple of films in a whole year, so naturally my heart grew heavy at the thought of going back home, disappointed. Perhaps it was the morose look on my face that made my uncle take me to 'The Albion'. Although the first talkie was made in Hollywood in 1927, Bengali films were still silent. I still remember the remarkable romantic scene of the wedding night that involved a close-up of the bridal couple rubbing their feet against each other. I also remember my uncle fidgeting in his seat—no doubt he was regretting having brought a young boy to see such a film!

Naturally, my first encounter with Bengali films did not prove to be a pleasant experience. That was possibly the reason why I do not remember having really wanted to see another Bengali film at the time. Besides, were films suitable for children made at all in those days? I don't think so.

'Ateet-er Bangla Chhobi', *Anandalok*, Puja Issue, 1978.

I started watching Bengali films only when talkies began in Bengal and films made by New Theatres Studio—bearing their logo that showed an elephant—became well known. Two of my uncles—Nitin and Mukul Bose—were, by then, well established as director, cameraman and sound engineer. Hollywood at the time was experiencing its golden age. In Calcutta, two cinemas opened their doors and created a major stir among film enthusiasts. These were 'The Metro' in 1935 and, a year later, 'The Lighthouse'. Both showed new films from Hollywood. What chances did Bengali films have when faced with the glamour and glitter of Hollywood stars, the power of their advertisements, the pomp of Hollywood films and clever cinematic techniques? Naturally, our films appeared lacklustre in comparison, and it seemed that we still had a great deal to learn. Sometimes one was inclined to think that although Bengalis had progressed a lot in art, literature and music, they were unable to grasp the special art of cinema— a gift from the West and an art highly dependent on machines and equipment—because it was simply not in their blood to do so. Perhaps they would remain unable to come to grips with it even in the future. To tell the truth, at the time Bengali films had to be watched with a totally different outlook; and the yardstick that was used to evaluate them was different from that used for foreign films.

In those days (I am speaking particularly of the first two decades after the talkies came) virtually every director—be it in Hollywood or Bengal—believed that a film was meant to be seen by everyone, and so it should please the audience from every strata of society. No one thought that cinema could be a serious art which might have room for deep philosophical ideas, fine sensitive analyses of psychological conditions, or complex characters with traits both good and bad, the kind of character one often finds in successful Bengali novels. Like Hollywood, Bengal had quite a few well-known writers involved with films. In the early days, I remember there were Premankur Atarthi and Saradindu Bandopadhyay. Premendra Mitra and Sailajananda Mukherji joined them later. The writer, Narendra Dev, wrote the first definitive book on cinema, in Bengali, as early as the 1930s. But even the involvement of such writers could not get Bengali cinema the status of art. This was primarily because even those writers did not regard cinema as a form of art. Those who have read the novel *Dampati*, written specially for cinema (by one of Bengal's best known authors, Bibhuti Bhushan Bandopadhyay), will agree with me. This novel gives a clear indication of what the writers of the era thought were the right ingredients for a film. Here I'd like to relate a personal experience. Once I went to one of our leading writers and expressed the wish to make a film from a story written by him. He sounded perfectly amazed as he said, 'But that story is true literature! How can you make a film from a story like that?' The truth is that cinema was then seen only as popular art; and a director made sure that he used just the right material needed for its creation.

It must also be remembered that in those days the number of films and auditoriums was very small, and the expectations of the audience were different. The formula now used in Hindi films, consisting of songs–dances–action–melodrama, was not yet born. Bengali films could be divided into three categories: social, mythological and religious. Of course, one cannot say that such a division cannot be made even today, and from what one has seen over the last few years, it does not seem that the expectations of the general audience have changed all that much. But having recently seen—on television and in cinemas—a few films made in the 1930s, I have come to believe that modern

Bengali films that fall into the above categories are of far inferior quality than those made before. Even in the early days of the talkies, the crew that worked in Bengali films (particularly at New Theatres) had mastered the technical aspects of film-making to a degree, showed an expertise in handling the camera, sound and editing, and dealt with the laboratory work with a neatness that I don't think can be found in many modern films. Judged in terms of those qualities, the old films seemed to have made quite a lot of progress.

It must be remembered here that it was not the age of realism. Hollywood at the time excelled in creating sets and artificial backgrounds. Most of the shooting was done in studios. Arc lights replaced natural sunlight. Roads, buildings, even gardens and woods were made within the premises of a studio. It made the work simpler, and the audience became used to that convention. Just as the audience in a theatre accepts the stage (a three-walled roofless structure) as a room or a house, those who saw old Hollywood films accepted their artificial surroundings. The only exceptions occurred sometimes in the 'Westerns' which showed wide open terrain where horses could gallop easily. Even Hollywood was unable to create such wide open spaces in a studio. In spite of the artificially created backgrounds, the best of the Hollywood films turned out to be really convincing and enjoyable on the strength of their scripts, acting and direction.

Unfortunately, Bengali films in those days did not possess these three qualities in full measure, so they failed to reach the same standards as Hollywood. Yet they directly copied various things from the latter. That became obvious particularly in the films that dealt with modern subject matters and social themes. A man would wear a suit and a hat or a dressing gown; a room packed with modern and trendy furniture would have a spiral staircase going up; the walls would be grey rather than white (or, in some cases, have wallpaper with floral patterns); a grand piano would grace the drawing room of people from the upper middle class, and the hero and heroine would play the piano while they sang—all these elements were copied from Hollywood. A number of popular and much acclaimed films of those times carried these features, notably *Didi*, *Jeevanmaran*, *Pratisruti*, *Mukti*, *Rajatjayanti*, *Doctor* and *Nurse Sisi*. The fact was that few directors had the courage to show the normal and ordinary lifestyle of Bengalis without giving it a veneer of 'westernized' sophistication. Yet I don't think any director ever tried to present an authentic portrayal of the westernized Bengali middle class that did exist in real life.

However, mention must be made here of one exception. The film *Bangaali* was made by Charu Roy when the talkies had only recently begun. I saw that film about ten years ago. I don't think I have seen any other film from that era that contained the same level of detail in the portrayal of life among the middle class. Unfortunately, I have not had the chance to see any other film by Charu Roy, although I have seen some stills from his other films which have led me to believe that Charu Roy was able to avoid the influences of Hollywood.

There were two categories of films that bore comparatively fewer marks of Hollywood. The first was religious films— such as Devaki Basu's *Vidyapati* or *Chandidas*; the other was films based on well-known Bengali novels—such as *Kashinath*, *Pallisamaj*, *Gora*, *Chokher Bali*—where faithfulness to the original story helped in keeping Hollywood at bay. But the 'Bengaliness' of these films is limited to their subject matter. There is no special quality in the language used in these films to suggest that the roots of that language lie in the earth of Bengal. This is because its source is Bengali theatre.

It is the influence of the theatre that led to the introduction of songs in Bengali films. There is no doubt that an arbitrary use of songs acted as a stumbling block in the way of Bengali films attaining full maturity. Songs may not be entirely irrelevant in films like *Vidyapati* and *Chandidas*, but if every director starts using songs in every film, one cannot but call it a national obsession. It was this obsession that turned a singer like Kundan Lal Saigal into a film hero—which made it possible for many a film made by New Theatres to make a lot of money—although his spoken Bengali was stiff and inadequate. The truth is that the audience in Bengal loves songs, and if it likes the songs in a film, it is prepared to overlook every lapse a director makes.

The films made in the 1930s no longer make an impact on our minds because of an absence of realism, the loose structure of the scripts, and stilted and artificial dialogue. Perhaps because of these reasons, the acting in these films—barring a few exceptions—also seems self-conscious and theatrical. In those days, Pramathesh Barua was well known for his restrained acting. Even today, it is acknowledged that his acting was free from the influences of the stage. If one isn't used to acting in plays, and does not have a very good command over the Bengali language, it is natural that his acting would not show traces of stage acting. It is likely that Pramathesh Barua could not have produced theatrical overacting, even if he had tried. Or it could be that his training abroad helped him to avoid the traditional mannerisms adopted by Bengali film actors. Barua was trained overseas to work in artificial light in a studio and had learnt about camera movements. It is difficult to say today whether, as a result of such training, he was able to make any new and startling impact on Bengali cinema—and, if he did, whether or not that helped to raise the general standards of films in Bengali. What *can* be said is that in films like *Mukti*, *Shesh Uttar*, *Shapmukti* and others, what strikes one today is not so much the mechanical techniques, but the overall 'hybrid' effect of the films.

It was in the 1940s that a new attitude was first seen in Bengali films. There is no doubt that *Udayer Pathay*—the film that created a bigger stir than any other at the time—was responsible for introducing that new attitude. The writer, Jyotirmoy Roy, was responsible for the social awareness one can see in its subject matter; but there are many other special qualities in the film for which the credit must go entirely to its director, Bimal Roy. He was the first to ignore the system of using stars and had the courage to bring in two completely new actors to play the hero and heroine. The situations shown in the film were far more realistic than in other films. The script was well-structured and the style of acting, as well as the way the story unfolded, was in keeping with cinematic norms. However, I saw the film recently and could not help feeling that even *Udayer Pathay* did not pass the test of time. The reason for that is the oversimplification of the characters and subject matter, and the kind of dialogue for which the word 'sharp' may be used, but which bears no resemblance to words spoken by real people in real life.

Bimal Roy made his best film *Do Beegha Zameen* in Hindi after he went to Bombay. A man who can claim to have made good films after going to Bombay—Bengali films, too—is Nitin Bose. His *Rajani* and *Noukadoobi* showed a lot more expertise than films made by New Theatres. The writer of *Udayer Pathay*, Jyotirmoy Roy, remained involved with cinema for quite some time, first as a scriptwriter, then as a director. The sympathetic portrayal of urban life in Bengal that was seen in *Udayer Pathay* was also seen in some of Roy's later films, such as

Abhijatri, Diner Por Din and *Shankhabani*. Sadly, I haven't had the chance to see them again to make a new assessment.

Among others who made significant films in Calcutta around the same time, three men deserve special mention: Hemen Gupta, Satyen Bose and Nirmal Dey. I happened to see Bose's *Borjatri* recently. Although it seemed a little immature in terms of technique, I could see that the passage of time had done nothing to diminish the pure Bengali mood it upholds, its amazingly natural and humorous dialogue (Bose showed great wisdom here by retaining, almost verbatim, all the original dialogue written by the author, Bibhuti Bhushan Mukhopadhyay), its spontaneous acting, and the appeal of numerous hilarious incidents.

Hemen Gupta's films, *Bhuli Nai* and *'42* had a major asset: the director's sincerity. Besides, both films can claim complete originality in their subject matter. One doesn't need to be told that the feeling of patriotism that runs through these films is the director's own—it is not borrowed from anywhere. It is this feeling that touches the heart of every viewer, in spite of various technical faults.

In my view, Nirmal Dey's *Basu Parivar*, *Sarhey Chuattar* and *Champadangar Bou*—made in the first two decades after the arrival of talkies—are the richest in qualities best suited to cinematic traditions, although there is no question here, either, of high-quality art or anything deep and meaningful. Like the film-makers of Hollywood at the time, Nirmal Dey sought chiefly to entertain various sections of society. But he handled his job with far more skill and good taste than most other directors. At the present moment, if Bengali films have to compete with Hindi ones, we need many more films of the kind that were made by Nirmal Dey. Pure art will never be enough for the industry to survive; at the same time, if Bengali cinema simply tried to imitate Bombay, it will only fall flat on its face. Of course, one needs to consider how many people there are today who can handle their work as well as Nirmal Dey.

Our country has always lacked stories well suited to cinema, as well as good scriptwriters. However, what we lack most today are directors who are familiar with every aspect of film-making and who possess a strong sense of responsibility. I do not know how such a void can be filled—yet if it isn't, we are in serious trouble. I am extremely doubtful whether financial assistance from the government alone will be enough to deal with this crisis.

6

Aspects of Art in Bengali Cinema

If one is to speak on the artistic aspects of cinema, naturally one must also consider the commercial aspects of film-making. I am a little embarrassed to raise the subject of money at the very outset. But it is true that without that one object, there is no way forward in cinema. A gift of the age of machines, this particular mechanical craft has assumed such proportions in the world of commerce that it has become impossible to make a film without spending a great deal of money. The basic materials required—a camera and film—are expensive enough. In addition, there are the actors to think of, salaries of other workers and technicians, renting a studio, making costumes and building sets. Even when a film is finished, there is no respite since one must then pay for advertisements and publicity. Taking everything into account, even a simple and straightforward film would require an amount in excess of a hundred thousand rupees. Something on a more lavish scale would naturally mean a higher figure. It is this dependence on money that has forced art to join hands with business and industry.

An artist knows that he needs money to give his ideas a

'Bangla Chalachitrer Art-er deek', *Betar Jagat*, October 1960, broadcast by Akashvani, Kolkata.

concrete shape; and a businessman knows that film-making is not something he can handle himself—that is the artist's job. Each has accepted his dependence on the other. The businessman—or the producer—raises enough funds, and the artist—or the director—makes a film with the help of those funds and hands it over to the producer. The producer then presents it to the general public through available cinemas. Only if the public accepts the film enthusiastically—that is to say, if they buy enough tickets and go and see it—can the film have any financial success. If commercial success complements artistic excellence, so much the better. But there is no guarantee that if you have one, you will also have the other. Many good films are not popular; and popularity amongst the masses doesn't always define artistic excellence. If that was the case, many of Tagore's creations could not have been considered as good literature. In a country where the spread of education is so limited, is it any wonder that connoisseurs of art should be few in number? Therefore, if a film is not commercially successful, its director need not think that he has failed as an artist.

However, a film's financial loss may well be cause for alarm for the businessman, i.e. the producer. For him, a film is successful only when it has made money. He is not really concerned with whether or not his film contains any aesthetic values. His first and chief concern is whether or not it is doing well financially. Since the director is dependent on the same businessman, how can he possibly overlook the producer's interests? A poet, a composer or an instrumentalist may have the freedom to work simply to satisfy their own creative urges, but not a film director. A director has to take care of the artistic as well as the commercial aspects of his work, bearing in mind the expectations of his audience. It would be most regretable if art has to be abandoned in order to meet those expectations. However, there are numerous examples in the history of cinema where popular demand and art have merged quite compatibly. Charlie Chaplin's films may be cited as examples. Of course, such amalgamation between the two is not easy, nor is there any formula for it. But since there have been examples in the past, there is hope for the future.

It is this hope that inspires those who try to make artistic films within the confines placed by commercial considerations. The best examples of successful cinema have all been created within those confines. There is, of course, a certain class of film-makers whose sole purpose is just to make a living. Who am I to suggest that such a purpose in life is either wrong or ignoble? But such directors cannot be included in any discussion on the art of cinema, for creating art is not their aim at all.

Let us now get down to the crux of the matter.

What *is* a 'good film'? Does it simply mean a film with a good story? I have heard many people say so. But if that is true, why is there such a dearth of good films in Bengal? So many films are based on good stories by writers ranging from Valmiki and Vedvyas to the best writers in modern times! The stories, by themselves, cannot be faulted. So what is lacking in these films that rob them of artistic success? The truth is that every story has two aspects—its underlying message, and its language. These two elements make up a story. The art of telling a story lies in the style that is adopted. A good story may be spoilt if it is not told properly; and a very ordinary story may acquire striking artistic features simply from the way it is related. The art of cinema is similarly dependent on its language and the manner in which the story unfolds. Where the language is weak, the film is unable to earn artistic merit. This language used in cinema is a language of images. A director must learn it and master its grammar. Even when he has done that it is impossible for him to work alone and express his meaning through that language single-handedly. Regular film goers will have noticed that a long list of credits appears on the screen before a film begins. It shows that the art of cinema calls for a joint effort. A film can be made only when a number of people work together. Some of them may be artists, some are artisans, and some others are both. They may be divided into two categories. The first would be those who face the camera, i.e. those who take part in the acting. The second would comprise those who remain behind the camera, i.e. workers in the background— the scriptwriter, director, cameraman, sound engineer, art director, composer and editor. Once a story has been selected, the first job falls on the scriptwriter. He turns the story into a format suitable for cinema. His job involves writing, but that kind of writing has no literary merit—or, at least, if it doesn't, it should not matter. The language in a script is only a written indication of the language that is adopted on the screen. The purpose of the script is to act as a 'skeleton'. As in a play, a story in a script is divided into acts and scenes. But there is a system of changing angles and changing shots virtually in every scene. This is completely different from a play meant for the stage. Such a technique is used only in cinema. Unless one studies cinematic grammar, it is not possible to master that technique.

As a matter of fact, it is both natural and desirable that the director should write the script. But sometimes a director is unable to write dialogue suitable for cinema, so he has to turn to a writer. The language that is hinted at in the script then has to be expressed through the use of a camera. The images that the camera captures are joined to one another, and only then does the story in the film take a finite form. Everything that is described in the story—the heroine's beauty, the hero's virility, the greenery of the countryside, the congestion in a slum, buildings, roads and alleys, wars and battles—all of it has to be seen through the eyes of a camera. A camera can certainly see as much as the human eye, sometimes a bit more. It has the ability and power to enlarge what is small, bring closer what is far, make an unattractive object look beautiful, and even turn day into night. That is why the camera is a director's biggest weapon. But its use involves dos and don'ts, right and wrong.

Whatever helps in highlighting the mood or theme of the story has to be seen as being right, and possessing adequate aesthetic merit. If the camera produces some special effects that fall outside the basic needs of the story, it can have no bearing on a general evaluation of the whole film. If the cameraman lacks an aesthetic sense or a sense of drama, he cannot possibly meet the director's requirements. His work remains limited to that of an artisan, and the language of the film is weakened in proportion to the cameraman's own shortcomings. Sound recordist, art director, editor, composer—each has to understand the requirements of the director, so that the work they produce fits in with the director's vision and the story finds its fullest expression. The success of a film lies very much in the success of these artists.

Let us consider the art director, for example. If he has to build a set to show the room where the hero lives, the appearance of that room, its size, its furniture, pictures on the wall, its neatness (or untidiness)—in other words, the total effect of that room must be consistent with that particular character in that particular film. If that is not the case, no matter how attractive the room is, or how well built, it cannot have any artistic significance. The same applies to acting. In Bengal, the tradition generally followed in acting belongs to the stage. On the screen, that kind of theatrical acting is not just unseemly, but also against all accepted norms of acting in films. The setting in a play does not reflect real life. A room with three walls on a stage is never acknowledged as a real room. That is why the speech or behaviour of characters on the stage cannot be the same as that of real people. No one even expects it to be so. But, in the realistic atmosphere created in cinema, theatrical overacting is most painful. However, it would be unfair to blame the actors for that. It is the director's job to judge a story and the characters in it, and then decide what kind of acting is suitable for each. He must have the sense not only to make that judgement for himself, but also communicate to the actors exactly what is required. It is up to the director to 'extract' from the actors performances that meet his own requirements. The director is responsible, to a large extent, for both the strengths and weaknesses of a film, as well as its artistic successes and failures.

That is something the viewers and critics must remember when they evaluate a film. If the story isn't good enough, the writer need not be blamed. Why did the director choose that story in the first place? If the acting is faulty, why did those faults escape the director? If the structure is weak, is that the fault of the editor, or was there a weakness in the basic structure of the script? Of course, in order to grasp where each mistake lies, one must be familiar with the systems and techniques used in cinema. Moreover, if a Bengali film is to be judged, one must also have a fair idea of the circumstances under which that film was made. There is no point in bemoaning the fact that bad films outnumber good ones. That is true of any work of art in any country in the world—and most certainly it applies to cinema. The truth is that, in the absence of a suitable artist, it is futile to expect the creation of great art.

Genuine talent is rare in any place, at any time. But in some foreign countries one may find the opportunity to study art; there are film schools where one may learn acting, direction or cinematography. It is possible there to see good films and analyse their language, grammar and style. Unfortunately, Bengal offers no such opportunity. There is no place where one may study cinema. In spite of that, one cannot help being proud of the success of Bengali films, the standard of acting and the expertise of their crew. I doubt whether, under similar circumstances, any other country would have achieved so much.

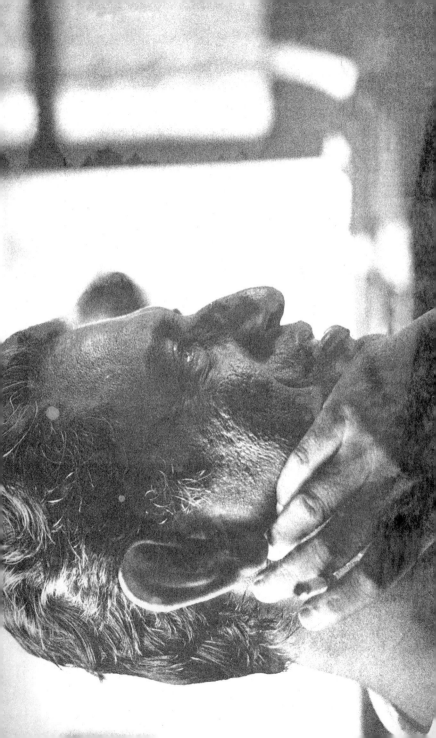

Indir Thakrun (Chunibala Devi) and Durga (Uma Dasgupta),
Pather Panchali, 1955

Young Apu (Pinaki Sengupta), *Aparajito*, 1956

Apu, the young man (Soumitra Chatterjee), *Apur Sansar,*
1959

Apu (Soumitra Chatterjee) and Karuna (Sharmila Tagore),
Apur Sansar, 1959

Apu (Soumitra Chatterjee) and Kajal (Aloke Chakraborty), the memorable final shot, *Apur Sansar,* 1959

Vishwambhar Ray (Chhabi Biswas), *Jalsaghar,* 1958

Indranath Choudhury (Chhabi Biswas) and Ashoke (Arun Mukherjee), *Kanchanjungha*, 1962

Charu (Madhavi Mukherjee), *Charulata*, 1964

Charu (Madhavi Mukherjee) and Amal (Soumitra
Chatterjee), the garden scene, *Charulata*, 1964

Bhupati (Shailen Mukherjee) and Amal (Soumitra
Chatterjee), *Charulata*, 1964

The memory game sequence, *Aranyer Din Ratri*, 1969

Asim (Soumitra Chatterjee) and Sanjay (Shubhendu
Chatterjee), *Aranyer Din Ratri*, 1969

The image of famine, *Ashani Sanket*, 1973

Somnath (Pradeep Mukherjee), *Jana Aranya*, 1975

7

Two Problems

Those who create literature find themselves unable to create anything new only when they run out of ideas, or have nothing left to say. Those who paint may have to make do with poor quality painting material, if one day good quality paints and brushes become expensive and scarce. If they cannot get paints, they can use chalk, and if even that is unavailable, there are pens and pencils. I have seen Nandalal Bose draw with twigs from a neem tree (used normally as toothbrushes).

Those who make a living out of art and literature can change their style of working and see how well it works out, if there is a drop in the demand for their own particular style. A change in style or method need not necessarily mean having to make a compromise. Even if there *is* a compromise somewhere, an artist's craft may suffer somewhat, but his entire livelihood need not come to a halt. It is true that external pressure *can* put a stop to all work, but that can affect any form of art and industry, in an almost identical manner. This is a well-known fact. Nothing new can be said about it. What I want to talk about are two problems that are wholly specific to cinema, and whose presence is being felt in Bengal more than anywhere else. One of these has rendered it impossible to make certain types of

'Duti Samasya', *Desh*, December 1967.

films; the other is either raising its head and becoming a stumbling block, or forcing one to look for a compromise.

Everyone knows about the new theatre groups in Bengal which are producing new kinds of plays. At the same time, some well-established groups are also experimenting with new subjects and styles—and even staging their efforts with considerable confidence. What this is resulting in is the virtual disappearance of a certain kind of traditional acting style. The style I am talking about came into being during the time of Girish Ghosh and found full expression in the acting of Sisir Bhaduri. It was not one uniform style of acting. Actors like Sisir Bhaduri, Naresh Mitra, Manoranjan Bhattacharya and Jogesh Choudhury were all contemporaries, all powerful stage actors nurtured in the same atmosphere; yet each had an individual distinctive style of acting. Nevertheless, although the crop it yielded varied, the land where it grew remained the same. A major reason for this was that these actors knew—and accepted—that acting is a form of art; and it can be expressed only by obeying the rules that govern it.

I am not suggesting that modern actors do not obey any rules. But the best acting in the past offered something extra—an authentic presentation of traditional Bengali values and behaviour, an all-round 'Bengaliness'. If that method had continued, it would have been possible to sustain that 'Bengaliness' simply through the same tradition of acting. It is this tradition that is on the verge of extinction.

For a film director, it is a huge loss because there are many characters one may think of which can come to life only through the old style of acting. It may be possible to make do with a new actor if the role is small and if his appearance and voice are more or less suitable. But if the character in question is Vishwambhar Ray of *Jalsaghar* or Kalikinkar of *Devi*, how is it possible to use an amateur? In such a case, there is no alternative but to turn to Chhabi Biswas.

Until Chhabi babu passed away, I had not realized that Bengali cinema was so dangerously dependent on him. Today, if I sit down to read a novel and come across the character of a powerful zamindar, or a refined, sophisticated, Westernized Bengali, I have to admit—with much regret—that there is no actor left in Bengal who can do justice to such a character. In fact, there is not a single actor who might merit the English term 'monumental', and be trusted to play such roles.

Tulsi Chakravarty's death has also created a void in a different field in Bengali cinema. Having a comical appearance isn't enough to be a successful comedian. It is possible to be a comedian like Tulsi Chakravarty only if one possesses a special comic sense and terrific acting prowess, in addition to comical looks. In the work of such a comedian, there can never be room for slapstick, though unfortunately, at times Tulsi babu was forced to resort even to that. There is no record of how many actors have become victims of a certain malpractice, both in cinema and the theatre, which calls for choosing one single aspect of the work of a multifaceted actor just because the audience likes it, and casting every performance in the same mould, thereby successfully putting a stop to the complete development of all his talents. Be it slapstick or true comedy, there is no one in Bengal at present who can take Tulsi babu's place. It is impossible, therefore, to portray on the screen several comic characters that one may find in literature. Come to think of it, would it be possible to make *Pather Panchali* today? No, because an actress like Chunibala Devi cannot be found every day.

Such are the difficulties these days in selecting a suitable story for film-making. In addition, another obstacle has now made its presence felt in the way of successful film-making (as well as selection of stories). I do not know how it might be removed.

I believe there are rumours afloat, suggesting that Satyajit Ray does not make films to show contemporary urban problems. I am sure everyone will agree that if a film has to be made about urban life it is necessary to show images of a city as well as its people. In other words, the action in the story cannot be confined to a studio, it has to be taken out and performed in the streets outside.

In the theatre, there has been an age-old tradition of events happening 'offstage'. Cinema rejected that tradition from the very beginning. Besides, in a film—particularly one that is supposed to show the problems of modern life—it is customary to be realistic. Therefore, any effort made to artificially create the streets of a city inside a studio is bound to fail. So the only way one can work is by taking a camera and shooting the necessary scenes out in the streets. Anyone who has tried to do that in the last five or six years will know just how difficult it is.

The fact is that, even though film-making is a regular discipline to the director and his crew, those who watch the whole process from outside often see it as no more than a tamasha; and if a popular actor is a part of that tamasha, so much the better. Who can resist the temptation of watching the goings-on in a free open-air 'theatre'? The minute a camera is set up anywhere in a city, or within ten miles of a suburb, great waves of humanity surround it.

The people who turn up do so not simply with a view to watching the shooting. Many of them nurture the wish to take part in the scene that is to be shot, i.e. show their faces to the camera. Those who do this are always hopeful of seeing their own faces on the screen at a cinema. I have tried explaining to them, time and again, that such good fortune can never come their way because no scene in a film will ever make room for anything that is irrelevant or unnecessary. My words do not seem to have the slightest effect.

In countries abroad, when a film is shot outside in the streets, the police step in to keep curious crowds at bay. In our country, it would create problems—rather than solve them—if the police were involved. In Paris, for quite some time, shooting in various parts of the city has been common practice, thanks to some New Wave film-makers. Parisians are so used to such a sight, or so conscious of the heavy damage they might cause if they crowded around, that crowds don't gather at all. I have seen films being shot, without the slightest interruption, even in a place like the Champs-Elysee. I have glanced around to see if there were policemen about, but never seen a single one. Such mentality from the general public cannot even be dreamt about in this country.

When I was making *Chiriakhana*, I had a set built to show Golap Colony in a suburb of Kolkata and thought I could work there in peace. While the construction work was being carried out, a garden was being put in place, rooms were being built and a compound wall was going up, no one interfered. But the day after our shooting began, at least a thousand people were seen arriving by train from different places. They poured in every day. Many of them would climb the wall and the mango trees behind it, simply to watch the tamasha. Even if they did nothing but spend all afternoon sitting in the blazing sun—men and women, young and old—they caused us a great deal of inconvenience and damaged our work endlessly. Then, when the sun went down, they would climb down from the trees and the wall and return to the station. Only the film unit knows how the work was eventually done.

We learnt something else from the experience: whatever else we may achieve, until the city dwellers in Bengal learn to think of the convenience of film-makers and grasp the enormity of financial risks involved in the entire business of film-making, as well as the scale of the labour employed, it will never be possible to shoot successfully, a film focusing on modern life in a city.

8

Background Music in Films

In the very early stages of cinema, i.e. when silent films were still in their infancy, so to speak, there was no such thing as background music. All that the audience could hear while watching a film was the whirring projector. When it became clear that such a noise was liable to interfere with one's enjoyment of the film, the system of playing a piano or an organ was introduced in cinemas in order to drown the noise made by projectors. Needless to say, it had to be ensured that the music was in keeping with the mood of the film. The pianists and organists that cinemas hired were responsible for matching their music to the film. The musician used his own intelligence and taste in music as he watched the film and played various tunes. As a result, different background music was imposed upon the same film when screened in different cinemas.

Griffith was perhaps the first director who became dissatisfied with this practice and found a new system. Griffith knew music, but was not a composer himself. So, instead of composing anything original, he chose suitable pieces from well-known composers such as Beethoven and Mozart. He wrote the entire score himself, and issued strict instructions to all cinemas to follow that score exactly as it was written.

'Aboho Sangeet Proshonge', *Desh Binodan*, 1964.

I do not know either the country or the film for which background music was first composed and an original score written; but in the silent era, the best-known background music came from the score written by the German composer, Edmund Meisel, for Eisenstein's film, *Potemkin*. According to contemporary reports, when *Potemkin* was shown for the first time in Berlin, the wonderful combination of moving pictures and music stirred the audience to a degree that had never been witnessed before. But Meisel's music did not get the chance to be widely known because it was composed for an orchestra. Few cinemas in the world had the means to keep an entire orchestra.

When the talkies came, the use of an orchestra to create background music became an integral part of film-making. Cinemas were no longer responsible for providing that music. Film producers themselves undertook to maintain orchestras. Every studio in Hollywood acquired one on a permanent basis. The best composers in Europe were attracted by American lucre and moved to Hollywood. They were quick to grasp what was needed and, within a short time, mastered the technique of composing background music for films.

For nearly twenty years after talkies began, this practice continued and no one questioned the use of orchestras. Gradually, however, a handful of films made in Hollywood itself began to deviate from the norm.

Carol Reed's *The Third Man* used only one instrument in its music: the zither. In *High Noon*, a male voice sang a cowboy ballad. In some films (*Boomerang*, *House on the 92nd Street* and *13 Rue Madeleine*, produced by Louis de Rochemont) it became evident that background music had been dispensed with altogether. That is when the established formula began to break up.

In the last ten years, the nature of film-making, as well as the methods adopted, has undergone a major revolution. A much wider range of subjects is now being used. Consequently, the style of narration, movement of the camera, editing techniques—all have changed. So has background music, in keeping with all these other changes. A modern composer knows that it is the theme or mood of a film that decides what form the music should take. It cannot be dictated by any set pattern, or rules laid down in a book.

A director's responsibility here is considerable. Who but the director would know enough about the mood that runs through the entire film, especially if its subject is new and so is its style? Whether or not background music is needed at all, and if it is, what its nature should be must be decided by the director. If a powerful director works independently and makes a successful film, it may be safely assumed that the background music in that film is based on the director's instructions. The composer must obey the director, since music in this case is not just a set of notes. Like the pianists and organists of yesteryear, a composer who works on film music today must have only one aim: to produce music that is consistent with the mood of the film.

It is not just the subject of the film through which this mood may be expressed. Different types of films may be made using the same subject matter, just as different writers can use the same story to produce literature that can be placed under different categories. Like literature, the class or category into which a film falls depends on its creator's outlook and the language he uses. The lines spoken by the characters, the style of their acting, the use of the camera, the rhythm and tempo of the film—all help in conveying a film's mood. Since composing the background music is a task that comes in the final stages of film-making, it should not be impossible for the composer to consult the director and, with his help, grasp the essential theme or the general tenor of the film.

There is one thing that a composer must remember at all times. A film has to be *seen*. What it would contain, apart from all the visual material, would chiefly be dialogue, as most of the story is described through words. A little more is expressed through sound effects. In this matter of telling the story, background music comes in last to do its job. This is so because although music has expression, it has no distinct language. There is, therefore, the need to make a suitable union between words and melody. Not all songs would work if they were set to the same tune. A song is successful only when its tune conveys the meaning of its words. Background music, if suitably used in a film, plays the same role of a 'conveyor'.

One question might be asked at this point: does a film need music at all? What could be lacking in a film that must be fulfilled by background music?

As a matter of fact, a director seeks refuge in background music only when he feels the need to highlight or heighten the emotional content in a scene by adding music to what has already been conveyed through the visual images, words and sounds. If background music is used without sufficient reason, it can only harm the film. It is also true that if there are faults and drawbacks in a film, the use of background music can do nothing to hide them. If, in a tragic scene, the director fails to strike the right note through other means, waves of even the most tragic and plaintive music produced by a violinist or a player of taar-shehnai will not cover that lapse.

A composer's responsibilities are much enhanced where the film's language is sharp and clear. An easy way to ruin a perfectly good film is to apply unsuitable music to it. A film made in a modern style and showing modern values may be spoilt if old-fashioned 'formula music' is imposed upon it. 'Sad music' in a scene where two characters are separated, 'happy music' where they are reunited, 'crash' at a moment of sudden melodrama, or 'suspense music' to emphasize tense and anxious moments are still used in our films. Perhaps there is no other alternative for films that have been made to fit a set pattern, but film-makers who work with new subjects and new styles have got to learn to abandon music of that kind.

The pattern that music in Bengali films has followed so far is a mixture of music from foreign films and jatra (folk theatre). The few jatras that I have been fortunate enough to see have led me to believe that the use of music in that form of theatre had once developed to the level of a fine art. Composers who worked in jatras realized a long time ago that it is not possible to create appropriate music for every dramatic moment by using only Indian instruments. Western instruments such as violins, clarinets, cornets and piccolos have been used in jatras for a long time. The melody played on these was based wholly on classical ragas. It never came to be regarded as high-class music because when Indian classical music is played on foreign instruments, the use of *sruti* and *meed* has to be avoided. But that does not really make any difference. Background music does not have to preserve the rigidity and discipline of pure classical music.

The composers in jatras have always worked towards one goal: to provide music powerful enough to compete with the loud voices of the actors and their most theatrical speech. With the exceptions of the sarod and the flute, all Indian instruments tend to produce soft and gentle notes. It is risky to use the sarod as there is every chance that the twang of its strings will clash with the hard consonants used in the dialogue, thereby distorting the music. The flute alone is not enough to deal with the musical requirements of the entire play. So jatra composers turned to Western instruments without hesitation. As a result, the great tradition of Indian classical music might have suffered a little, but the composers' task in providing appropriate music became easier.

In the matter of background music, it is meaningless to worry about rules laid down for singing or playing pure classical music, as background music need not be assessed as pure music at all. It is possible to create rhythm and melody by playing any instrument, and so anything on earth that will produce the right note may be used. For one of my own films, Ravi Shankar created music by playing upon not just a sarod and a pakhawaj, but also pitchers, bowls, even cups and saucers. In a formal musical gathering, such an attempt would imply not simply a deviation from tradition, but sheer madness. However, if the background music it provides can match the mood of the film, it is not just music, but music that has been entirely successful in achieving its goal.

The truth is that, in films, it is virtually impossible to find the chance to use classical ragas in their pure and undistorted forms. Every raga has its own entity. If, in a film, a raga familiar to the audience is played in the background in the traditional manner, it will soon begin to distract the audience and make their mind leave the film to wander off into the world of classical music. It is easy enough to see that, should this happen, the background music will have failed to accomplish its mission. However, having said that, I must admit that many films have made partial use of ragas, with a great deal of success. Some composers tend to show certain partiality towards particular ragas, which is natural. There are ragas that are eminently suitable for conveying particular moods, both amongst people and nature. For instance, one might look at ragas played at dawn, although in the kind of lives that we lead today, the possibilities of catching that particular moment when dawn breaks are becoming increasingly rare. But no one who has stepped into the open air and witnessed the appearance of the first light under perfectly natural conditions—and felt its glory with his entire being—would ever doubt the incomparable powers of ragas such as Lalit, Bhairon, Todi, Ramkali and Khat to convey that special feeling.

The same may be said about evening ragas. In the whole day, perhaps the most meaningful moment—to anybody's mind—arrives at that juncture when day gives way to night. That is why ragas such as Sree, Puravi and Dhanesree have been so amazingly successful in arresting the sad, melancholy air of the twilight hour. Other hours of the day do not have a clearly defined character. A raga like Sarang therefore does not automatically remind one of an afternoon; nor does Behag bring to mind thoughts of the night.

Among the six seasons, the two most poetic and distinctive—*vasant* (spring) and *varsha* (the rainy season)—have been caught and expressed most clearly through various ragas. Needless to say, what they reflect are the emotions these two seasons arouse in people's minds. A film composer turns to these ragas to express the same feelings.

I shall now quote a few instances from my own experiences before finishing this essay. From *Pather Panchali* to *Charulata*, the business of background music caused us several problems, which we tried to solve as best as we could. *Pather Panchali* was set in a village, but that did not mean that its story could be seen as folklore. There was an unmistakable sophistication in its language and treatment; and there was evidence of modern psychological thinking in the description of its characters. In the film, attempts were made to portray similar sophistication. We did not therefore think that anything could be gained by confining its background music to folk tunes played on rural instruments. That is why Ravi Shankar did not hesitate to use the sitar, sarod and pakhawaj, in addition to a flute and ektara.

The Postmaster (the first part of the film *Teen Kanya*) was also set in a village. But in this story, the style, the mood and even its subject matter were all very simple. So we did not find it necessary to use more than three instruments to create its background music—a flute, do-tara and sarinda.

In *Jalsaghar*, what decided the nature of its background music was the aristocratic and feudal spirit of the film. There is a historical link between pure classical music and the special atmosphere that runs through the story. We are all aware of such a link. The composer, Vilayat Khan, used most skilfully a variety of classical ragas on such instruments as the sitar, surbahar, sarod and sarangi.

While the music for *Jalsaghar* was being created, we learnt something new. It turned out that even when the background music is based on classical ragas it is not advisable to use a tabla as accompaniment. The sound of a tabla immediately suggests a musical soiree, and the mood it evokes ruins the real purpose of the background music to a great extent.

We learnt something else. It was simply that although our background music was based on classical ragas, we were not obliged to follow all the traditional norms. If it is felt that the mood of the film comes through adequately when a raga is played in its undistorted form, that is exactly how it ought to be played. However, on many occasions, as one mood shifts to another in a particular scene, it becomes necessary to move from one raga to another. A skilful serving of a concoction of ragas can create an amazingly dramatic mood. Every music connoisseur is conscious of that. A composer working in a film should be able to capture that dramatic element in various ragas and use it beautifully to his advantage.

There may even be moments when a sudden discordant note in a given raga may work much better than anything else in order to underscore those moments. There is no cause for hesitation here, either. What may appear disrespectful and unacceptable in a live concert can easily become appropriate and even artistic in a film. The main thing is that the composer must remember that here his loyalty lies with the art of cinema, not the traditions of music.

When I made *Mahanagar* and *Kanchanjungha*, I encountered some new problems. The story of *Kanchanjungha* revolves around a particular class of people in Bengal. They belong to the upper middle class and some of them are overtly westernized in the way they dress, speak and behave. The action takes place in the town of Darjeeling. There are the mountains on one hand and, on the other, the stamp of Western culture in the behaviour of these people. These two elements acted as the chief source from which emerged the background music of *Kanchanjungha*. Local pahari folk tunes were broken and altered wherever we wanted, and played on both Indian and Western instruments—solo at times, or as an ensemble.

Like *Kanchanjungha*, the chief difficulty in *Mahanagar* lay with the problem of fusion. The central figure in this film is Arati, a housewife from a lower middle-class family. It is her job that takes her from her home into the world outside. This is followed by scenes from the ever-changing city, from its streets, trams, buses, restaurants, an Anglo-Indian colleague's house, to the smartness of a posh area like Alipore and a sleek, modern, air-conditioned mercantile firm. Each of these images keeps returning. Apart from that, there is mental turmoil and conflict within the character, a sub-plot concerning the old father-in-law and many other factors. Not only did the scenes change swiftly, but there was a plethora of different components that went into the film. So I thought it would not be right to lumber the film with a complex background music and tax the audience further. In the end, what little music was used was provided only in the interest of the unfolding drama, and to create an appropriate mood.

Among the films in which I took on the responsibility of composing the background music so far, I think the music in *Charulata* has turned out to be the most spontaneous and well-applied. The main reason for this is the experience I have gained over the years. Experience matters a great deal in working on a film's background music. Even when one has a fairly good idea of the theme or mood of a film, it is not easy to know which instruments should be played in a particular scene, or which melody, rhythm and tempo should be used to best effect. That is the reason why, even now, mistakes and lapses occur when composing the music for a film. There is plenty left to be learnt, especially in a place like Bengal where people's lives, their clothes, their speech, even the houses they live in do not have a clear and distinct character, everything is a great medley. Against such a backdrop, it is extremely difficult to compose the music for a contemporary film. Yet this challenge cannot be avoided.

Abroad, various interesting scientific experiments are being carried out in music. Musical instruments have been discarded altogether and, with the help of sound engineering, electronic music is being created through an artificial process. Obviously, that kind of music is not going to be suitable for all types of films. Instrumentalists need not therefore worry about their future. But these experiments are opening up new avenues for film composers. In an age that is changing so rapidly, it is naturally impossible to make any final comment on the art of cinema, but one thing may be said for sure. In India, the problem a composer of background music must face is not one to do with the paucity of material; it is to do with its abundance.

9

Dialogue in Films

The films that we generally tend to see are realistic in nature and dependent on dialogue. There *have* been films—even after talkies began to be made—that have been devoid of spoken lines; but those are so few and far between that they cannot be treated as part of the established norm. There are some films, such as cartoons and musicals, or films based on fairy tales and other purely imaginary stories, that do not require realistic dialogue. But we hear—or hope to hear—realistic dialogue in most of the films we see.

The role of dialogue in a film is twofold. First, it explains the story. Second, it describes various characters in the film. The same function that words perform in literature is performed together by images and words in a film. Words are not needed to describe a scene; images can do that job. When it comes to describing the physical attributes of a character, again images can handle that. It is the nature of the character that comes across partly through the expression and gestures made by an actor and the rest by words he or she speaks. One ought to try to convey through words only what images cannot capture. A new scriptwriter does not always remember this;

'Chalachitrer Shanglap Proshonge', *Anandabazar Patrika*, Puja Issue, 1963.

hence his work often becomes riddled with an excessive use of words. It is an extremely difficult task to gauge accurately the extent to which words should be used. Once a scriptwriter has learnt to make that assessment, his way forward becomes a lot simpler.

In Bengali films, there has been a long-established tradition of using melodramatic dialogue. That kind of dialogue is really more suitable for the theatre. Words are all-important in a play, not in a film. The situations often described in plays have so little to do with situations in real life that the audience does not even expect the characters in a play to speak the natural and realistic lines that one may speak in real life. Dialogue in a play therefore takes an oversimplified and overtly dramatic form, in keeping with the equally dramatic situations.

Scriptwriters in our country frequently forget the difference between plays and films. The lines that the hero and heroine speak, in particular, are far more suited to the theatre than to cinema. At times, the story demands that these characters should slip from the straight and narrow. Their feet slip, but their speech does not stumble even once.

If there is no spontaneity in the dialogue, it is difficult to produce natural and spontaneous acting. In real life, one might deliver the same lines differently under different circumstances. Certain words may be spoken in a certain way during a moment of idleness; and in another, during a busy moment at work. As a matter of fact, even when the words remain the same, the way they are spoken when one is hot and sweaty on a summer day will be distinctly different from the way they are uttered on a day in winter when one may be shivering with cold. When a person is relaxed, his tone is slow and measured. In a state of agitation, words get disjointed, sentences are spoken between short breaths.

The difference in class between two people results in a difference in the language they speak. Educated Bengalis usually speak a mixture of English and Bengali. Since the country's independence, some people have acquired the habit of avoiding English words, but they are small enough in number to be regarded as negligible. It is therefore entirely natural to use English words in the lines spoken by an educated Bengali.

What is perhaps most important about scriptwriting is that the writer should forget his own identity completely, enter the character he is describing and, through the use of dialogue, bring that character to life. Another important thing to remember is that, in a film, time is of the essence. If a lot can be expressed through few words, nothing like it; and if, instead of words, a gesture can be used, so much the better.

There are many writers in Bengal who are highly skilled in writing natural and realistic dialogue, although it isn't always possible to use their lines in a film without making a few changes. However, if a scriptwriter wishes to learn how to write such lines by studying literature, I can recommend one writer without the slightest hesitation. He is the late Bibhuti Bhushan Bandopadhyay. No other writer can be looked upon as a guru in the matter of writing dialogue for a film script. Conversations in his writing sound as if he picked up sentences directly from people in real life and put them down on paper. His lines fit the characters so well, they are so revealing that even when the author provides no physical description, every character seems to present itself before us simply through the words it speaks. It is not possible to write dialogue like that without extraordinary powers of observation, and a remarkable memory. Needless to say, it is essential that a scriptwriter should possess these two qualities.

10

Films in Colour

When talking of *Ashani Sanket*, many people have asked me why I chose to use colour to make the film. After all, when I made *Pather Panchali*, based on a novel written by the same Bibhuti Bhushan who wrote *Ashani Sanket* and which was a story about poverty in a village, it had not been necessary to use colour; then why use it to tell the story of a famine? A question like this indicates the ideas and beliefs held by the general audience about the use of colour in cinema—that colour is inextricably linked with glamour and therefore the painful existence of people in the lower strata of society cannot be successfully portrayed through its use. Such an idea isn't unnatural. Even a few years ago it was the generally accepted view. Even those who were closely involved with cinema believed that a serious subject and colour did not go together. Nobody abroad holds such a view any longer; but in our country, people who have seen colour only in Hindi films, or are not familiar with the restrained use of colour in serious foreign films, are very likely to harbour such an idea. Before I go into *Ashani Sanket*, I need to say something broadly about films made in colour.

Everyone knows of the revolutionary changes brought

'Rongeen Chhobi', *Desh Binodan*, 1972.

about in the late 1920s by the introduction of sound in cinema. While it is true that silent films were a distinct art form, it must not be forgotten that in order to narrate the story, even silent films had to resort to using written sentences from time to time. Such sentences appeared as titles inserted between scenes. They were used only when visual images alone were not enough to explain an event or action. In the talkies, dialogue replaced titles. Attempts began to be made to use spoken words to describe those facts related to the story—or a character— that could not be conveyed merely through acting and visual details. At first, both the dialogue and the acting were theatrical; but gradually it became more natural and transformed itself into a purely cinematic style. It was then widely acknowledged that, with the inclusion of sound, cinema had come very close to real life.

Then came colour. In the real world, colour and sound both exist and cinema draws its materials chiefly from the real world. What is remarkable is that just as in the silent era no one complained about the absence of sound, nobody seemed to regret the absence of colour even after the talkies came. Even so, improvements in technology led to the birth of colour films. The first commercial colour film, *Becky Sharp* (in which three colours were used), was released in 1935. Though the use of colour was a novelty that startled and enchanted the audience, no one seemed to think that the inclusion of sound was also responsible for creating a revolution in cinema. Shortly afterwards, Eisenstein and other theorists discussed the various possibilities involved in the application of colour, but I do not think those discussions made a wide impact at the time.

After *Becky Sharp*, films in colour gradually increased in number; but, at the same time, black-and-white films continued to be made. Over a period of time, a certain formula emerged with regard to the use of colour. Musicals with songs and dances, historical films with a lot of pomp and pageantry, fantasies, children's films, light-hearted romantic comedies, or anything that included beautiful natural scenery, would all be made in colour; and films with a serious theme, or spine-chilling thrillers and detective films were going to continue in black and white. This became a practice in Hollywood. It is not difficult to guess from this that at the time even Hollywood was not able to accept that colour could be used to make a serious film. Only ten years ago, I realized after talking to some foreign film-makers that they too thought colour was suitable for relatively light subject matters. They had accepted the complete disappearance of silent films; but, in the age of talkies, they were not in the least desirous of seeing black-and-white films sent on a permanent exile as a result of the dominance of colour films.

Today, however, that practice in Hollywood and the views of those film-makers have changed totally. Like silent films, black-and-white films have reached the point of extinction abroad. The chief reason for this, of course, is a commercial one. The expenses and complications involved in making a colour film today are much less than before. Secondly, the general audience prefers colour. Thirdly, after the introduction of colour on television, colour films have found a new avenue through which they can make money. For these reasons, some foreign film-makers today are more or less forced to make films in colour. And for similar reasons, they are also forced to think afresh about the stylistic aspects of applying colour to films.

As a result of this new thinking, everyone has come to the conclusion that the addition of colour has undoubtedly enriched the language of cinema, and there is no subject for which the use of colour is inappropriate. It is not just that film directors are agreed on this. No film critic in foreign countries today will complain against the use of colour in a particular film. What everyone is concerned about now is simply the aesthetic merits of the application of colour.

The truth is that just as the misuse of sound had prevented cinema from being treated as a serious art form in the early 1930s, ten years later a similar misuse of colour made colour films remain as outcasts in the matter of gaining artistic recognition. In the early stages, the main aim of those who were thinking of using colour was to establish a direct connection between cinema and paintings. A similar motive made black-and-white films use chiaroscuro—a conscious use of light and shade—that was related to paintings. In the early colour films what is noticeable in the application of colour pertains to the art of painting. When Korda made a film based on the life of Rembrandt, he made a conscious effort to use Rembrandt's well-known favourite colours in most of the visual material. In recent times, a similar tendency is evident in films made about Lautrec or Van Gogh. It is not difficult to find other examples, in addition to lives of artists. Rouben Mamoulian's *Blood and Sand* was set in Spain. Mamoulian decided that the Spanish painter Velasquez was to be his ideal and followed the latter's style in the use of colour.

At about the same time, art directors in colour films were seen performing a new role, that of a 'colour expert'. Now their job was to obey the rules of colour harmony and choose the furniture and costumes accordingly; and cameramen aimed to display those colours to their best advantage by a skilful application of light. Even when shooting a scene in natural surroundings, in the matter of composition and colour, attempts were made to adhere to the traditional practices in painting. It goes without saying that many of the early films bear evidence of refinement and sophistication in their use of colour.

However, in spite of all this, it has to be said that such an application of colour cannot be deemed successful if cinema were to be judged as an art form. It is true that cinema has a relationship with the art of painting. In certain films—particularly a few made by Eisenstein and Dreyer—this relationship is made very clear. But in ninety per cent of the films that are made, the mobility of the camera and visual images wipe out every relationship with the still composition of a painting. In such films, therefore, it is meaningless to use colours that would normally be used in paintings.

What one has to realize is that only if colour can be used as an intrinsic part of the language of cinema will its use be successful. To make their use in films worthwhile, it is not enough if colours in a film merely demonstrate a refined taste in their selection. A truly artistic application of colour began when film-makers realized that colours could play a special role in explaining the story, describing characters and the atmosphere, creating the right mood and adding a dramatic effect, or simply presenting facts. If today, directors abroad have voluntarily started to make films in colour, it is because their decision to do so is based on that realization.

II

Among the various means that a director can adopt to convey a meaning or present a fact, the weakest is words. A scriptwriter turns to words only when visual aids and sound prove inadequate. At least, that is the norm of all successful films. Every film-maker has to remember the Chinese proverb, 'one picture is worth ten thousand words'. The chief skill of a capable director is to make a scene speak volumes even without taking the help of words. The movement of the camera, acting, visual details, editing—all of these can combine together to achieve that goal. Another thing that can help is the use of colour.

Before speaking further about colour, let me give a few examples of the limitations of black and white. In black-and-white films, it is virtually impossible to make a distinction between white and pale colours, or black and other dark shades. I remember reading a review of *Pather Panchali*, in which the critic had complained that, in a scene related to a wedding, I had shown the bride wearing a black sari. The sari, in fact, was red. Similarly, it is impossible to distinguish between gold, silver, copper, bronze and aluminium. Yet suitably chosen objects like jewellery, furniture and utensils can certainly help in amplifying certain facts in order to take a story forward. The vermilion in a woman's hair cannot be shown unless the film is in colour. *Alta* (a red liquid) on a woman's feet turns black. A sari with a broad red border loses its special significance. Subtle and fine descriptive details of the beauty of nature in rural Bengal—to which Bibhuti Bhushan draws our attention time and again—cannot be captured unless colour is applied.

A cloudless sky changes colour every few hours. Sometimes it is dark blue, at other times it is pale, or all traces of blue may disappear altogether to leave it a clear white; at dawn and dusk there would be hints of yellow, red, orange and purple. Every situation evokes a different mood; every stage is capable of creating a special feeling at a particular moment in a film. But it is possible to show that only through colour.

There is no doubt that colour can also enhance various traits in a character. It is not difficult to portray in black and white the difference in class between one character and another; but when using colour, these differences can be highlighted much more easily and sharply. Even here, what is used is the ability of colours to convey a message or information. In *Kanchanjungha*, there were eight or nine main characters. While choosing their clothes, an attempt was made to hint at their individual position in society, each individual's taste and even state of mind. In a black-and-white film, such a task could have been handled only partially. The rest would either have remained unspoken, or words would have had to be used to explain the full meaning.

Colours can also play an important role in creating a dramatic effect. A painter may avoid a clash of colours on his canvas in the interest of good taste. A director, however, can use such a clash beautifully to produce an element of drama.

In contrast, sometimes there is a restrained use of colour. The subject and theme of a film may demand that the colours be soothing and subdued. The audience may even forget temporarily that they are watching a colour film.

The horrible effects that can be produced by an intemperate use of colour can be seen in any Hindi film made today. Colour is used in Hindi films purely for glamour. Glossy and multi-hued packaging is necessary to hide the weaknesses in the basic subject matter. No Hindi film-maker shoots in a natural environment unless there is a bright sun. That, too, is related to considerations for glamour. Yet it is perfectly possible to shoot on a cloudy day and catch its melancholy solemnity, even in colour.

I am reminded here of my experiences while shooting *Kanchanjungha*. A Hindi film was also going to be shot in the same place, at the same time. Bearing in mind the weather conditions in November, provisions had been made in the script of *Kanchanjungha* to include cloud and mist as well as sunshine.

The Hindi director was going to shoot a song sequence. In the twenty-six days that we took to finish shooting *Kanchanjungha*, we took every possible advantage of the swiftly changing natural conditions. In those twenty-six days, the director of the Hindi film failed to shoot even that one song sequence simply because he had to wait for the sun to come out.

After completing the shooting of *Ashani Sanket*, I truly believe today that colour is suitable for any subject. Like every other component that goes into a film, the main function of colour is to speak—but not more than is necessary; nor is it supposed to overshadow the basic message of the film. Whether a film is showing poverty or wealth is quite immaterial since poverty has its own special colour, as does wealth. Besides, like sound, colour is a part of the real world. If the use of sound in cinema is appropriate, there is no logical reason why the application of colour cannot be the same.

11

A Critic in the Eyes of a Director

What I am going to say about the relationship between a film critic and a director will reflect only my own personal views. Generally speaking, I do not know whether my views have any significance.

Prior to the release of *Pather Panchali* in 1955, film critics did not know me as a director. In other words, *Pather Panchali* was made without being influenced by film critics in any way. If criticism were to have any effect on my creations, that would have happened after *Pather Panchali*. But since most film critics have continued to say that *Pather Panchali* is my best film, a question naturally springs to mind: hasn't the effect of criticism been beneficial to my art?

In order that such a question does not confuse any critic, I should state at the outset that I do not think comments from critics have made any impact on my films. If, in the last ten years, my art has really not improved at all, only I am to blame.

Some new and inexperienced directors may certainly gain from comments of judicious critics who may point out flaws and suggest how they may be rectified. However, if the director as an artist is conscious of what he is doing, he will not be unaware of the strengths and weaknesses of his creation. He

'Parichaloker Drishtite Samalochak', *Desh*, Puja Issue, 1965.

will then deserve praise for the merits and blame for the demerits in his work. But if the critic cannot substantiate his praise or criticism with appropriate evidence, his criticism will only irritate the director. A director does not expect to be told anything new about his own work. What he does expect is endorsement of his personal views as reflected in that work.

One may well ask here whether such endorsement has any value for the director. I would say that it has enormous value. I may make a film in my own style, following my own ideas; if a critic has the perception to grasp the essential message of the film, how can I deny that he acts both as a friend and a person with real insight?

A critic earns the right to analyse the merits and demerits of a film only when he has a true understanding of the art. He must know and be able to judge every aspect of film-making, from writing the scenario to its editing. In other words, he must always remember that cinema is a joint venture. The director may be in supreme command, but he can never claim 100 per cent credit for all the merits of a film. On the contrary, he may be held responsible—to a far greater degree—for all its drawbacks. It appears from the comments of some critics that they do not have a single clear idea about this 'joint' aspect of film-making. 'The script is skilfully written' yet 'the dialogue is weak'; or 'the direction bears a masterly touch' yet 'the editing is ridden with errors'—one comes across such contradictory remarks from time to time. Dialogue is always a part of the script, and if editing is faulty the director must share the responsibility.

Only those who are closely associated with a film are in a position to judge who deserves any credit or blame (and in what proportion) for a film's strengths and weaknesses. It is therefore dangerous for a critic to apportion either blame or credit. From a director's point of view, that may even become totally laughable. The critic might proclaim that the spontaneity in so-and-so's acting is remarkable. The director, however, is aware that behind the actor's spontaneous acting lies the director's long-drawn and tireless efforts, and most—if not all—of the credit should go to him.

In countries abroad, it has been long recognized that if a novel or short story is to be adapted into a film, it may be necessary to make certain changes to it, in the interest of the art of cinema. But in our country, critics have not yet been able to accept this artistic requirement. That is why, after I made the Apu trilogy and films based on Tagore's short stories, I had to put up with severe chastisement from critics. Every time, it seemed to me that just because they had recently seen the film versions and had copies of the original stories ready at hand, these critics completely ignored their real duties and simply filled their columns by quoting the dissimilarities between the two and making various irrelevant but seemingly deep and meaningful remarks.

In my view, a critic performs a useful purpose only when he is able to build a bridge between the director and the audience. That is his main responsibility. A critic has to be a connoisseur since he makes a living out of making appraisals. However, unless a viewer is prompted by a personal motive, there is no reason for him to want to become a true connoisseur. Where a film is simple as well as good, the critic's responsibility is diminished because the viewer can appreciate its excellence without the critic's help. But there are some films which can be understood and appreciated only if the viewer has the necessary knowledge and perception. In such a case, a critic has to step in and perform the role of a teacher.

If a critic harbours the view that 'good' automatically means something the general public can grasp easily, I certainly would advise him to leave the job of a critic and become a viewer. Every director, motivated by his artistic and creative urge, has the right to remain a few steps ahead of his audience. This 'being ahead' need not necessarily mean following a path that leads to good or serious art. The artistic merit in the director's work must be assessed by the critic. What he has to do is walk together and keep pace with the director, grasp the essence of his art and convey it to the viewers. Today, when film-making is undergoing such enormous and rapid changes, and new experiments are being made virtually everywhere, a critic must keep his senses alert at all times in order to make an objective assessment of new methods and new styles. Even the definition of a story is changing today. Thanks to progress in science, there have been revolutionary improvements in most equipment. The range of subjects has expanded so much that even Joyce's *Finnigan's Wake* has now been made into a film. A modern critic therefore has to perform a very difficult task. Nevertheless, he can be of particular help when a director decides to go down a path no one has walked on before.

Does a critic have any say in whether or not a film will do well commercially? Only a Gallup poll can answer that question. However, in this connection, I can quote something from my personal experience. Anyone associated with the film world in New York believes that the lifespan of a film hinges largely on the views of the film critic of the *New York Times*, Bosley Crowther. When *Pather Panchali* was released in New York, Crowther wrote that the film was thoroughly unsuitable for the New York audience. Those involved with the distribution of the film became worried. But, contrary to expectations, *Pather Panchali* ran for thirty-four weeks in the city of New York alone. Perhaps Mr Crowther learnt a lesson from that bitter experience. So, when *Aparajito* came along the following year, he praised it sky-high. *Aparajito* ran for just eight weeks.

12

On *Apur Sansar*

In the review of *Apur Sansar* published in *Desh*, 16 May, the critic has praised it sky-high in the beginning and at the end ('. . . in its mood, feelings and style, this film will remain an eternal prize possession for Bengali cinema' etc), but somewhere in the middle, he has quoted lines from the original novel with a view to proving various weaknesses in the film's script. Whether or not the script suffers from inconsistencies, the apparent inconsistencies in the views expressed in his article by the critic, Chandrasekhar, are most surprising.

From the lines quoted from Bibhuti Bhushan, it becomes quite clear that the critic has read neither *Pather Panchali* nor *Aparajito* with care; or else the only intention behind quoting those lines was to belittle the script of *Apur Sansar*.

The critic has said, 'Perhaps it is in this film that the mismatch between the author's vision and the director's imagination has become more obvious than in previous films.' An author's vision is expressed through words; a director's imagination (even when based on a novel) is revealed mainly through moving images. Doesn't the critic realize that the two are as different

'*Apur Sansar* Proshonge', *Desh*, 30 May 1959.

as chalk and cheese? No film based on a novel has yet been made which did not require the director to use his own vision and imagination.

Yet according to the critic, 'The director takes recourse to his own vision in establishing the central character in a way that does nothing to indicate a successful manifestation of that vision.' I don't think there are any basic differences between the Apu in the novel, and that in the film. On the contrary, the Apu who exists in the critic's own imagination seems to bear little resemblance to the character Bibhuti Bhushan describes. Two things have got to be remembered regarding Bibhuti Bhushan's Apu: (a) Apu's character shows a complex mixture of various elements, and (b) Apu is a lot more sensitive than most people, i.e. he is moved more deeply than others by both grief and joy. According to the critic, 'After Aparna's death, Apu has been shown as a bearded man weighed down with grief, who roams in various places over a period of five years, carrying the pain of his loss everywhere. In this attempt to lengthen the film by harping on Apu's grief, it is difficult to find Bibhuti Bhushan's Apu.'

The novel does, in fact, very clearly describe how deeply Aparna's death had affected Apu's entire being, and for how long. Bibhuti Bhushan says, 'What a huge emptiness, what a colossal loss he had suffered, it could never be redressed in his entire life. Nothing, no one, could fill that void. There was nothing before him—no trees, no creepers, no flowers or fruit . . . only an endless expanse of dry, hazy, sandy desert.' (Mitralaya edition, page 230.)

A year after Aparna's death, Apu thought of leaving his home in Calcutta because 'there were so many memories of Aparna associated with that house—it became impossible to continue to live there' (page 232). Then, again, on page 234, he says, 'Apu could no longer live in Calcutta. Everything about it had become totally intolerable. Besides, a baseless and unreasonable belief was slowly taking firm root in his mind: everything would be all right if he could get out of the city.' After this, there is a description of how Apu moves to Chapdani and begins working as a teacher. Two years after Aparna's death, Pranav and Apu meet here. Bibhuti Bhushan says, 'Apu was no longer the person he had once known, Pranav thought. The young man who used to brim with the sheer joy of living, now seemed dull and lifeless. Why, it had never been in Apu's nature to show such crude instincts and be so easily satisfied with his lot!'

The contrast shown between Apu's optimism and his will to live when the film opens, and his bitterness, roughness and cynicism after his wife's death, is based very much on Bibhuti Bhushan's own description.

The critic makes another peculiar remark: 'The way Apu keeps (his son) Kajal at bay as something "untrue" and "unreal" also hampers the mood of the film.' Has this critic read the original novel at all? In it, this is what Apu happens to be thinking about Kajal two years after Aparna's death: 'Apu had always felt strangely displeased with his son, possibly because he had unconsciously blamed him for Aparna's death. He had thought of visiting him during the Puja holidays, but when the time came, he felt no real urge to do so. Only his sense of decency made him send five rupees by money order to buy the child new clothes, thus fulfilling his parental duties.' (Page 245.)

Apu went to see Kajal for the first time almost a year after this event and that, too, only for a few days. The critic in *Desh* has remarked, 'The sweet relationship between Apu and Kajal that is described in the original story is barely visible in the film. Kajal's failure to recognize his bearded father results in a failure to present the audience with a glimpse of what the author describes.' Bibhuti Bhushan describes Apu's first meeting with Kajal in the following manner: 'At first Kajal refused to come to his father, the sight of a stranger made him cling to his grandmother. Apu felt a little hurt.'

Even after having met his son, Apu felt no great affection for him. He left him again and disappeared into the unknown. When Kajal turned five, Pranav saw him one day and realized the little boy's helplessness. This is the comment he made against the absent Apu: 'What a heartless wretch! Where has he disappeared to, and left this poor little motherless child with no one to take care of him? . . . Is he totally devoid of any compassion, any pity?' (Page 288.)

Three years later, Apu returns to Bengal from Madhya Pradesh. Instead of going straight to see his son, he first goes to Calcutta. He is far more keen to get news of his friend, Leela, and is in no hurry to visit Kajal (page 300). Several months pass before he visits Kajal ('Apu could not recall what his son looked like . . .', page 319). When he sees Kajal for the second time, this is how Bibhuti Bhushan describes his feelings: 'Today—the minute his eyes fell on Kajal—a great ocean of love began welling in Apu's heart . . . how *could* he have neglected him all these years?' (Page 320.)

The critic has also made a comment about Kajal killing a bird in the film. His comment suggests an absence of common knowledge as well as ignorance about the original novel. Anyone with even some simple, basic knowledge about child psychology would know that the tendency to be cruel is natural and not uncommon amongst children. Bibhuti Bhushan has mentioned this more than once in his writing, and written about it even in his diaries. The truth is that the incident regarding killing a bird was taken from the novel, *Aparajito* itself, except that the incident in the novel centres around not Kajal, but Apu (then five years old):

> Durga saw what had happened and said, 'Give it to me, let me look at it.' Then she picked up the bird and inspected it curiously. Its neck was broken, blood had oozed from its mouth. Some of it got smeared on Durga's finger. 'Why did you have to kill it?' Durga scolded him. Apu, who had been feeling quite victorious, suddenly felt a little deflated.' (Page 45.)

The critic might well say that this little incident spoils the sweet innocence of Apu's character. There is hardly any need to point out that the mentality shown by Apu is all the more natural and applicable to an orphan like Kajal. According to the critic, however, 'Kajal's behaviour makes it difficult to believe that such sadism (!) can come from Apu and Aparna's child.'

There is one more thing: Bibhuti Bhushan's Kajal is not simply 'imaginative, meek, nature-loving'. According to the author's description, 'he could not keep still for a moment, he was always restless; nor could he keep silent. He talked non-stop' (page 313). His grandfather imposed strict discipline on him and, if necessary, beat him mercilessly (page 313).

The critic has noticed an absence of tenderness in the relationship between Apu and Kajal, as described in the screenplay. In fact, the sweet and tender note on which the screenplay ends with a union between father and son is just the opposite of how the original novel ends. In the latter, Apu leaves Kajal in the care of his childhood friend Ranu, and goes overseas.

'You must stay here, Khoka; if I left you here, couldn't you do it? Would you like to stay with your auntie?'

Kajal said, 'Leave me here by myself? No, never! I will go with you, Baba!' (Page 376.)

Apu did not grant his son's request.

If the film continued with the story even after father and son had been united, and went on to deal with their final separation (including their visit to Nischindipur, where they met Ranu), heaven knows how long it would have become. One wonders whether it would then have exceeded the optimum length of a film that is worth screening, and whether such a long film could have met all the artistic demands of good cinema. Perhaps the critic can throw some light on this matter?

There are one or two other critical remarks in the article, but I see no reason to either comment on or protest against them, since a critic has the right to offer his own views (good or bad) independently, on any film. Only one thing needs to be emphasized: what the relationship has ever been between a novel and film, what it should be, or can be, is something that our critic needs to study in much greater depth. There is no dearth of examples of successful films that are based on novels. If the critic has no faith in home-grown material, he can still learn a lot from foreign classic films.

{13}

On *Charulata*

I opened the October issue of *Parichay* and discovered that Mr Rudra is after me again. The problem is that cinema has become an art for all and sundry. Normally, only those who appreciate—or try to appreciate—excellence in paintings, books and music would feel the urge to visit exhibitions of good paintings, read good books or go to reputed live concerts. But in the case of cinema, I often find that anyone who has seen *Sangam* will also peer into a screening of *La Dolce Vita*. There is nothing, of course, that one can do about it. If someone has a rupee and twenty-five paisa in his pocket and about three hours to spare, he can see any film he likes and comment on it. I have no problems if his comments are confined to gatherings at the Coffee House or local clubs. But if every Tom, Dick and Harry starts to reveal his little and, therefore, dangerous knowledge in journals and magazines, a question arises quite naturally: will it not create confusion in the minds of at least a certain number of readers and viewers, especially when film goers in Bengal have only recently started showing an interest in learning about cinema, and displaying signs of being able to distinguish between good and bad films?

I do not know if Mr Rudra understands anything of

'*Charulata* Proshonge', *Parichay*, 1964.

literature. Of films he understands nothing, but it is not just that. He doesn't understand even when things are explained to him. In other words, he is totally beyond redemption. He may have seen some good films abroad. But who has told him that anyone who has seen good films can automatically appreciate them, or has the right to write about them?

If the truth be known, it is writing that is Mr Rudra's obsession. This is what he has written about *Charulata*: 'The similarity that Mr Ray's *Charulata* bears to Tagore's *Nastaneer* is the same as the similarity it bears to thousands of other stories in the world.' It is my belief that if I had changed the names of all the characters in *Charulata*, as well as the period in which it was set, and released the film claiming that the original screenplay was my own, Mr Rudra would have immediately grabbed the special centenary edition of Tagore's complete works and written a long essay (perhaps for no other journal than *Parichay*), complete with quotations, simply to prove me a plagiarist.

In his present essay, Mr Rudra has discussed three of my films that were based on stories by Tagore. I am going to limit myself to *Nastaneer* since I believe that this one example will highlight the difficulties in making a film from a piece of literature. Needless to say, not every story requires the same number of changes. In foreign literature, there are many good stories (for instance, the stories of Chekov and Maupassant) that read almost like ready-made screenplays. *Nastaneer* does not fall into the same category of stories. Why that is so—I hope—will become clear later in this very article. Therefore, when Mr Rudra asks, 'Was there any problem in keeping the story completely unchanged when the screenplay was written?' it becomes apparent that he needs to be taught the basic a-b-c of scriptwriting.

Mr Rudra speaks of the 'well-structured and cohesive' plot of *Nastaneer*. In my view, the plot in that story is of secondary interest. If that was not the case, it would have been possible to relate the 'story' of *Nastaneer* verbally, without hampering the flow of the original text. Perhaps Mr Rudra would care to try his hand at such an exercise? The chief asset of *Nastaneer* is the psychology of its four main characters and the very sensitive and sympathetic analyses of their relationships. Various incidents are described in order to portray these relationships. The main thread of the story emerges from these incidents. However, the event that is used to take the story to its final conclusion is bound to appear both sudden and artificially imposed, because Tagore does not offer even a hint of Umapado's betrayal, either through dialogue or an incident in the story.

Let us look at the story from its beginning.

Tagore describes Bhupati thus: 'Bhupati had no real need to work. He had enough money, and his country was warm. But, through a twist of fate, he was born as a man who sought useful employment. Hence he was obliged to publish an English newspaper.'

The mock-serious tone of these lines is maintained throughout the story. It was an entirely conscious decision on Tagore's part to choose this particular tone for this particular story. An analysis would show that without such a tone, it would have been impossible to use these four special characters and make this special story sound convincing.

The first 'event' in *Nastaneer* is that of Umapado talking Bhupati into starting a newspaper. Bhupati remains so deeply engrossed in his work that he fails to see 'when his child-bride Charulata slowly stepped into youth'. If the film was to start with the emergence of the newspaper, Charulata had to be shown as a young girl; and a number of extra scenes had to be included to show Bhupati's involvement with his paper and Charu turning into a young woman. I do not know what Mr Rudra would have said about those extra scenes, but perhaps even he will agree that such scenes would have meant a weak start for the film. So I decided to start by showing Charu's loneliness.

An important question arises here: was Amal brought up in Bhupati's house? Tagore mentions Charu's loneliness *before* the first mention of Amal in the first chapter: 'In that wealthy household, Charulata had no job. She was like a flower that blooms to perfection, but does not go on to bear fruit—her only job, through every long day and night, was to try to emerge as a distinct entity despite all the lack of need for her self, and absence of any effort.'

A little later, we learn that Charu would 'catch Amal and get him to explain her lessons to her'; and 'Amal made endless demands just because he taught her a little. Sometimes, Charu pretended to get cross about it and even rebel against Amal; but to feel that she was of some use to someone, and put up with his affectionate tyranny, had become essential for her'.

These lines point to a stage when—to a certain degree—Charu has learnt to deal with her loneliness and lack of close contact with Bhupati, by making friends with Amal. Therefore, if the film was to start with Charu's loneliness, Amal could not be shown immediately. He had to arrive later and a new scene had to mark the moment of his arrival.

What we tried to show, in addition to Charu's loneliness, was her passion for reading, interest in crafts, an inherent childlike quality in her (without which it would have been difficult to show her growing friendship and compatibility with Amal later on), Bhupati's engrossment with his paper and indifference towards his wife, and Charu's acceptance of her husband's behaviour. Apart from all this, we aimed to hint at the specific period and atmosphere.

The next important event in the story is the arrival of Mandakini, Charu's sister-in-law. In the original text, this is how the reader is prepared for Mandakini's appearance: 'When a female relative drew his attention to his young wife and scolded him a little, Bhupati suddenly became aware of the situation and thought, yes, Charu ought to have another woman for company; she has nothing to do all day, poor thing.'

If Tagore had written *Nastaneer* as a screenplay, I doubt very much whether there would have been any room in it for this unspecified female relative. In cinema, such vagueness can never be allowed. At the same time, a completely new character could not be introduced with the only purpose of 'drawing Bhupati's attention' to his wife. So what did one do? Here is an example of how a scene, based on the original text, might have been written in a certain kind of film that is partial to theatrical speech:

Bhupati (stuffing food into his mouth): By the way, I met Pishima today. She mentioned you.

Charu: I see.

Bhupati: Do you know what she told me?

Charu: What?

Bhupati: She said that after having spoken to you the other day, she has realized that you are very lonely.

Charu: Never! I didn't say such a thing to her at all.

Bhupati: Even so, she has felt your loneliness.

Charu: Never mind all that. Would you like some more puris?

Bhupati: And yet, *I* never thought of it? How strange! How unfair! Really, such a lapse is quite unpardonable.

Charu: Are you going to eat, or just talk nonsense?

Bhupati: I am going to tell Uma to bring Manda here.

In my view, it wasn't altogether impossible that at some casual moment, Bhupati should guess, unaided, that Charu was lonely. No matter how well Charu hid her feelings, there had to be a limit to it; and even a busy and inattentive man like Bhupati could not be totally devoid of sensitivity. Besides, in the original story, there is nothing to suggest that Bhupati was unsympathetic towards his wife.

In the film, the afternoon shown in the opening sequence and the night that followed in the second scene were supposed to reflect a typical day in the lives of Bhupati and Charu. The original story mentions a large number of unrelated events and incidents, spread over several days and several nights; but there is not a single scene—complete in every way—that involves both husband and wife. One may not be conscious of the absence of such a scene while reading the story. But because time, place, characters and atmosphere—everything takes a concrete shape in a film, and the story proceeds from a certain point in time, it becomes important to show a scene like that. The audience is bound to feel curious about how a busy man who neglects his wife when he is working might treat her when he is not. For that reason, too, the first night scene became necessary.

In the first part of this scene, we see Bhupati having his dinner. Charu is sitting in front of him, a palm-leaf fan in her hand. Bhupati tells her of his intention to appoint Umapado manager of his newspaper. In the original story, there are just three references to Umapado. First: '(Bhupati's) brother-in-law, Umapado, gave up trying to make a go of his career as a lawyer and said to his sister's husband, "Bhupati, you should bring

out a newspaper in English. You have such extraordinary ...'"
Second: 'Umapado was explaining how different gifts should
be offered to the readers along with the newspaper. Bhupati
was finding it most difficult to understand how those gifts
could possibly wipe out his losses and bring in some profit.'
The first reference makes it clear that Umapado is a failed
lawyer, but it gives the reader no reason to suspect his character.
The second reference suggests that Bhupati and Umapado are
having a difference of opinion about the general policy in
running the paper, but it is nothing serious. Yet, when the third
reference comes up, we see immediately that Umapado has
betrayed Bhupati's trust.

In the film, like the other four characters, Umapado simply
had to take on a concrete form. How could his betrayal become
convincing if there was no hint of his weakness either in his
own behaviour, or through conversations about him between
other characters? Also, unless it could be shown—through
events or dialogue—that Bhupati was placing his trust in his
brother-in-law, how could the latter's betrayal shock and move
the audience?

Having considered these factors, we decided to show that
when Bhupati appoints Umapado as his manager, he does so
with an awareness of Umapado's weaknesses—partly because
he is Charu's brother (and therefore worthy of Bhupati's trust),
and partly because Bhupati appears to want to reform him.
Charu herself implies that her brother's character isn't unknown
to her ('Can Dada do it? He can never settle down to a job!').
In Tagore's story, there is no indication of what Charu and
Umapado think of each other; nor do Amal or Manda ever
mention Umapado. Yet he plays a most important role. In the
film, therefore, his role could not remain hazy, nor could his
character remain in the background.

After the scene showing Bhupati at dinner, the same sequence continues and shows a much later hour. Bhupati is busy writing his editorial. Charu comes and stands at the door. In her hand is a handkerchief, embroidered specially for Bhupati. Bhupati looks at Charu.

Bhupati: Two minutes, Charu.
Charu: I didn't come here to hurry you.

The story is still in its early introductory stage. At this stage, Charu cannot get cross or impatient with her husband. If she could, the story of *Nastaneer* would have taken a different form. Charu comes forward and hands the handkerchief to Bhupati.

Bhupati: *You* made this?
Charu: Now I'm going to embroider your slippers.
Bhupati: Where do you find so much time, Charu?
Charu: Time isn't something I lack, is it?

Charu only hints at her loneliness and moves to the next room. She doesn't want conflict between Bhupati and herself over this issue. Besides, it could be that she doesn't even expect Bhupati to take her hint.

But Bhupati does not fail to get her meaning. He thinks for a while, handkerchief in hand, and says, 'You feel quite lonely, don't you, Charu?'

'Oh, I've grown used to it.'
'To be used to loneliness isn't a good thing, Charu!'
'Have you read *Swarnalata*?'

Charu asks this irrelevant question here to test how closely aware Bhupati is of her loneliness. If one irrelevant question leads to a complete change of subject, Charu has no hope of getting Bhupati's continued attention. That a reserved yet sensitive woman like Charu should test her husband in this manner struck me as fully consistent with her character.

Bhupati does not hear her words clearly.

Bhupati: What?
Charu: *Swarnalata*.
Bhupati burst into laughter.
Charu: Why are you laughing?
Bhupati moves closer to Charu and puts his arm around her.
Bhupati: I have my own Charulata. Plays, novels, poetry—I want none of those. Do you understand?
He moves Charu towards their bedroom, his hand still on her shoulder. The last words he speaks in this sequence can now be heard.
Bhupati: I'll do one thing. I'll tell your brother to bring your sister-in-law with him. Then you won't lack company, will you?

This is where the first phase of the film comes to an end.

The second phase starts with another afternoon. Manda is lying on Charu's bed and playing a card game with her. In the original story, various comments about the character of Manda are sprinkled here and there, just as there are comments about all the other characters: Manda is 'obtuse', 'whatever her virtues, she lacked imagination' etc. In other words, in Manda, Tagore offered an almost direct contrast to Charu. So it was impossible for Manda to be a suitable companion for Charu, or remove the emptiness in her heart. Charu yawns as she plays, and either snaps at Manda or remains silent when Manda tries to joke or even make a serious remark.

In Tagore's story, the events that show Charu and Manda

together all involve Amal. Yet if Bhupati's plan has to fail, that scene between Charu and Manda is absolutely essential. In the film, Amal arrives the same afternoon, soon after the scene showing the two women playing cards. The original story does not have a scene at all to mark Amal's arrival; hence, here the director has to depend purely on his own imagination.

In the interest of economy, care was taken to be as brief as possible in explaining the Charu–Amal relationship. Amal arrives just as a storm is breaking. He tucks his umbrella under his arm and touches the feet of his bouthan (sister-in-law). His first words are 'Bouthan, have you read *Anandamath*?'

Charu's fondness for Bankimchandra Chatterjee, the writer of *Anandamath*, has been established in the first few scenes of the film. Amal's remark therefore implies their common taste in literature.

As soon as he has finished greeting Charu, Amal runs off to look for his cousin, Bhupati. Charu is pleased to see Amal, but there is nothing to suggest anything more than that at this point. The simple pleasure Amal and Charu feel in seeing each other merges with the rising storm. The excesses provided by nature prevent the duo's emotions from appearing exaggerated.

There is nothing in the original story that describes a meeting between Amal and Bhupati. Hence there is the need to use one's imagination again, and be economical. Amal touches Bhupati's feet, promptly picks up Bhupati's teacup and sips from it, as if he has a natural right to use his cousin's property.

Bhupati: How is pishima?
Amal: Don't ask! It was Ma who delayed me. She just wouldn't let me go.

It was necessary to show exactly how Amal and Bhupati were

related, so 'pishima' (father's sister) had to be brought in. Such
things in a film can be explained only through dialogue—unless
Mr Rudra is aware of an alternative.

Bhupati threatens Amal with a task: he would have to check
the proofs. This is mentioned in the third chapter of the original
novel. Then he shows his young cousin the printing press he
owns. His newspaper, *The Sentinel*, is shown being printed
(in the novel, the newspaper must have had a name, but Tagore
did not mention it). Bhupati is in the process of writing an
editorial on the government's border policy. Amal pretends
to be scared: 'You've cast aspersions on the government?' (In
the first chapter of the novel, there is mention of Bhupati's
editorial on the same subject.) Amal can do no more than make
light-hearted comments on politics as it is a subject that does
not interest him.

When Amal leaves, Bhupati and Umapado discuss some
affairs related to the newspaper. In Tagore's novel, there is a
suggestion that the two had a difference of opinion over the
management policy of the newspaper, but there is no full-length
scene, complete with dialogue, to focus on that issue. I don't
think it is possible at all to write a screenplay from a story like
Nastaneer without including such a scene because, as I've said
before, unless Umapado's betrayal is convincing, the intensely
tragic conclusion of the story cannot be convincing. Besides,
it was necessary to inform the audience that Umapado was
'the general manager of Bhupati's paper. He was in sole charge
of collecting subscriptions, settling payments owed to creditors
and paying the employees' (chapter 9). Tagore reveals these
details only when he describes Umapado's betrayal. Tagore's
style would not have suited the purposes of cinema. But not
only were those details extremely important, it was also vital
to let them be known, clearly and strongly. It was for this reason

that a scene was included in which Bhupati hands over his keys to Umapado.

In the third phase of the sequence that begins in the afternoon, Charu and Manda are both shown in Amal's room. This brings together all the main characters who would eventually go through the stresses and strains of a 'pentagonal' relationship before taking the story to its end.

In that early scene in Amal's room, when Charu and Amal are shown, there is not even a hint of anything more than the simple, sweet relationship that normally exists between a brother-in-law and sister-in-law. Amal speaks as he starts unpacking; Charu stuffs his pillows into their cases. If Mr Rudra had watched this scene carefully, he could never have made such a totally erroneous comment as 'Charu stares at Amal throughout with glowing eyes'.

The scene ends with Charu snatching a torn shirt from Amal and taking it away to mend it. There is no reason to believe that such behaviour shows anything other than Charu's natural instinct to act as Amal's guardian.

The night scene that follows brings the film's exposition to an end. In this scene, we see Amal with Bhupati, not Charu. It is important here to remember the lines that Bhupati speaks in the third chapter of Tagore's novel: 'Amal, I am so tied up with my newspaper, poor Charu is left totally on her own . . . you, Amal, if you can keep her engaged in reading, that will be good . . . Charu is quite interested in literature.'

In other words, Tagore *wanted* Bhupati to act as an agent who brings Charu and Amal closer together. A scriptwriter would naturally avail himself of this golden opportunity to use the irony in the situation.

However, in the original story, long before Bhupati makes this request, 'Charu catches hold of Amal and gets him to help her with her studies' (chapter 1). When Bhupati makes his request in chapter 3, Amal does not reveal that he has already helped Charu. Instead, he says, 'If Bouthan starts studying, I believe she can learn a great deal.' Neither in the novel nor in the film is there any suggestion that Amal is delighted by Bhupati's request. The joy and enthusiasm come more from Charu than Amal. In the film, when Bhupati makes that request, Amal says, 'Dada, am I going to study literature, or get your wife to do so?'

The 'development' phase of the film starts right after this. It needs to be stressed here that the exposition has already indicated the form the film's main structure will take. Instead of following the different events and dialogue that are scattered throughout the novel, each taking place at a different time, the script follows the age-old tradition of scriptwriting and takes the story forward through complete and discrete scenes. The reason for this is not simply a whim on the part of the scriptwriter; the opening sequence showed how it became imperative to resort to this measure. Certain methods were adopted, in keeping with established cinematic norms, to create that opening sequence. If those methods and norms were abandoned or ignored in subsequent scenes, *Charulata* would certainly have failed as a work of art.

A few other reasons must be given here to stress why it was impossible in the film to follow the original text word for word.

In the novel, various events are described that take place 'daily', or 'sometimes', or 'occasionally', or 'from time to time'. For instance, 'sometimes Charu pretended to be cross, and rebelled . . .'; 'Amal reminded her daily and demanded . . .'; 'occasionally, Amal read his essays at literary gatherings'. Anyone with even a rudimentary knowledge of film-making would know that most of these events that occur 'sometimes' in the novel could not be shown in the film 'from time to time'.

In addition to these, there are descriptions of some other events in the novel which may be brief, but hint either at long passages of time or important developments in the story. For example, Charu expects that Amal's essays would not be read by anyone except the two of them. Amal, however, cannot resist the temptation of seeing one of his essays printed. He sends it to the *Sararooha* magazine. When it is printed, he himself tells Charu about it very proudly. After that, 'Amal began to have more of his essays published. He received praise . . . sometimes even letters from admirers. He showed them to Charu. Just occasionally, he got an anonymous letter from a woman. Charu teased him about it, but she did not feel pleased. One day, when he found a spare moment, Bhupati said to Charu, "I say, I had no idea our Amal could write so well!"'

If all these stray occurrences had to be accommodated in the film through different scenes and dialogue, how could the story maintain an even balance? Would Mr Rudra like to think about it? Even if the original story was faithfully followed, the scriptwriter would have had to invent new dialogue and new scenes. No doubt Mr Rudra would have objected even to all of those.

What really needs to be considered is this: once all the essential changes and deletions have been made in the interest of giving the film a satisfactory structure, how similar—or otherwise—is the story in the film to the original novel? Are the theme, plot and characters changed and transformed to such a degree that the similarity the film bears to *Nastaneer* is the same as the similarity it bears to thousands of other stories? The answer to that question, I believe, will become clear by the time this article is concluded.

In the film, the 'development' or 'middle' stage starts with events on another afternoon. In the first afternoon shown in the film, Charu is alone; in the second she is with Manda; the third shows Charu, Manda and Amal. A short summary of the third scene is as follows: Charu is working, Manda is just whiling away her time; Amal arrives clutching a book, on Bhupati's instruction, to discuss literature with his Bouthan. At Amal's request, Manda goes and brings some paan. Amal ignores her request to play a card game and starts talking about literature. Charu gets involved in a literary debate with Amal; Manda falls asleep. The sound of her snoring disturbs the other two, so they pick up a mat and leave for the garden. Before she leaves, Charu puts down the object she has been working on. It is a half-finished embroidered pattern for Bhupati's slippers. Until that moment, she does not stop working. What Mr Rudra calls 'staring at Amal with glowing eyes' is not shown in this scene, either, since the time has not yet come when Charu would neglect her wifely duties in order to enjoy Amal's company.

In the original novel, there is no complete scene that introduces the individual relationship between these three characters; nor does any of the dialogue used in this special scene feature anywhere in Tagore's story. Therefore, if anyone looks for an exactly similar scene in the original, they will not find it. Even so, I must stress that there is nothing in this scene that might suggest a distortion of this particular triangular relationship. If anything has been changed or added, it is purely for the sake of compression.

About the scene in the garden, Mr Rudra has said, 'The friendship between Charu and Amal that emerged through their plans of rebuilding the garden is absent in the film, because this primary relationship is evident in Tagore's theme, not in Satyajit Ray's.' How strange! In the story of *Nastaneer*, long before plans regarding the garden are mentioned, there is mention of Charu and Amal's friendship in Charu asking Amal to help her with her studies, Amal making demands on her time, and Charu embroidering a pair of slippers for Amal. But, in the film *Charulata*, it is in the garden that Amal and Charu are first shown together without a third person; and it is here that they talk freely with each other.

In the film, events on three different days are shown in the garden. The first day marks the beginning of their friendship; on the second day, Charu takes advantage of that friendship to make a demand on Amal ('Whatever you write should remain in that notebook. You mustn't have it printed!'); the third gives the first hint of turmoil in Charu's mind. Bhupati is absent throughout in this phase. Manda is present, but only as a spectator, as she is in the original text ('Will you please bring a ripe plum for me?' is all she asks).

In *Nastaneer*, the conflict that arises over the Charu–Amal–Manda relationship has been summed up in these few words: 'A person seeking refuge in a household does not look kindly upon another refugee.' Manda, therefore, does not pay much attention to Amal at first. But once Amal becomes an acknowledged writer and 'when Manda saw that Amal was getting a lot of respect and admiration, she too raised her face and looked at his proud bearing. The glow of pride and success on Amal's young face brought enchantment to Manda's eyes— it was as if she looked at him anew'. (Incidentally, the reader cannot be blamed if such a description makes the reader think that, like Charu, Manda is neglected by her own husband and is therefore attracted to Amal.)

'As a result, it became difficult to keep Manda at a distance', because Manda began feigning an interest in literature, and Amal began spending time with her without thinking at all about how Charu might react. Naturally, Charu is upset by his behaviour. She starts writing herself, only to prove how much more intelligent than Manda she is. After much struggle, when she finally overcomes Amal's influence on her writing and finds her own style, the literary merit in her writing certainly exceeds Amal's. (It is not difficult to see the sarcasm in Tagore's tone when he describes the titles of Amal's essays, their subjects and language; but Charu's writing proceeds a little only 'when her language and style both began to reflect the pure simplicity of life in a village'. Amal, however, thinks that 'the article began well, but the poetic element in it could not be maintained through to the end'.)

Nevertheless, he insists on sending it to a magazine in order to placate Charu. When it is printed, a critic in his review praises Charu's essay much more than Amal's. At first, Charu is pleased, but feels worried that it might hurt Amal. When Amal finds Charu with the review, he thinks just the opposite: 'Charu is overjoyed just because I've been abused and she's been praised sky-high.' Amal goes off to find Manda, which intensifies Charu's anguish. She goes to Bhupati and complains, 'I've been watching Manda's behaviour for some time, and I don't like it. I'm now scared to keep her here.'

The character of Amal, as it emerges through these events, is at once immature, vacillating and weak. In her plea to have Manda removed, even Charu's character is undermined and she behaves with unexpected crudeness. Tagore was able to create a suspension of disbelief amongst his readers even when he described this series of events, partly by taking the advantages available naturally to a writer of literature, and partly through his own eloquent language. No film-maker could possibly achieve what Tagore did. The directness adopted in cinema would have prevented these events from being convincing and, as a result, the number of misunderstandings between Amal and Charu and the degree to which one feels hurt by the other's actions would have seemed quite artificial. Throughout the film, the audience would have been plagued by a single question: why are they constantly holding things against each other, when they are being given every opportunity to talk things over and clear the air?

Yet it cannot be denied that these childish misunderstandings are a very important part of the first phase of the story. The inevitable tragedy of the final conclusion is heightened greatly if it can be seen against the background of such simple childishness. Bearing that in mind, as well as the possible reaction of a contemporary and modern audience, certain changes were made to this section of the story.

I thought it would be natural for Charu to feel upset if she learnt that Amal was spending time with her largely because Bhupati had told him to do so. In the film, that marks the beginning of Charu's pride being hurt. Amal takes advantage of the situation and adds insult to injury by seeking Charu's permission to send his article to a magazine. In the original story, there are many instances of Amal's insensitivity regarding the nature and degree of Charu's pain.

Amal leaves the garden, comes upstairs and, having failed to find Charu in her room, goes off to find Manda. 'Which magazine should I send my article to?' he asks Manda playfully. He knows that his relationship with Manda is such that there can be no awkwardness over feelings being hurt or intentions being misunderstood. Charu hears the last few words spoken by Manda and Amal. By then Amal is back on his feet and walking away. Charu finds a small and silly excuse to scold Manda.

What the 'drama' in the story demanded next was that Bhupati be involved in these cross-currents. In the original, Bhupati fails to notice—time and again—the real nature of the tensions between Charu and Amal, although it was he who acted as an agent to bring them close, in the first place. It was this factor that had to be highlighted in the film. In addition, Charu's hurt pride had to be soothed. The ideal way to achieve both ends, I thought, would be through a scene that talked of a marriage proposal for Amal.

In the novel, this event takes place *after* Umapado's betrayal. It is necessary here to quote a few lines from Charu and Bhupati's conversation from the novel:

> Bhupati: Wouldn't it be better if *you* first reasoned with him before I said anything?
>
> Charu: I have already spoken to him, three thousand times. He doesn't listen to me, I can't speak to him again.
>
> Bhupati: Do you think he won't marry?
>
> Charu: We've tried so many times before. He's never agreed to marriage, has he?
>
> Bhupati: But this time, he really shouldn't refuse this offer. I have a large number of debts to repay—I can't go on providing for Amal as I have done.

What is worth noting here is that Bhupati is interested in seeing Amal married partially to ease his own financial burden. In the novel, Amal accepts the proposal for marriage. The previous chapter hints at the reason for his acceptance. After Umapado's betrayal, Amal notices Bhupati's 'pale and stricken' looks and asks Charu what is wrong. Charu replies, 'Why, I didn't notice anything! May be some other journal has called him names.' It is at this point that Charu's insensitivity suddenly opens Amal's eyes to the real situation: 'Amal cast a sharp glance at Charu's face—what he saw, or what he felt, one doesn't know. He rose quickly to his feet. It was as if a traveller, walking through clouds and mist, had stopped as the mist cleared and realized with a shudder that he was just about to step into a gorge, a thousand feet deep.'

In the period between his agreeing to get married and actually leaving for the ceremony, Amal made enquiries and 'learnt about (Bhupati's) predicament. Then he thought about Charu—he thought about himself—his ears turned red—he shouted loudly, "To hell with the *Moon in the Sky* and *Light on a Moonless Night*! If I can return as a barrister and help my brother, only then can I call myself a man!"' (There are some innocent readers who see nothing other than a sweet and affectionate relationship between Charu and Amal, perfectly normal between a married woman and her husband's younger brother. I ask those readers to pay particular attention to the business of Amal's 'ears turning red'!)

At this juncture, the scriptwriter must think over the following facts:

(a) After Umapado's betrayal, Manda and Umapado are obliged to leave Bhupati's house and return to Mymensingh. Don't Charu and Amal feel even slightly curious about the real reason behind their departure? Should they remain totally indifferent about this matter? The audience might well find their indifference hard to believe.

(b) As a result of Umapado's betrayal, Bhupati appears 'pale and stricken'. The sight of his face makes Amal grow anxious about him. Only a few minutes before Amal sees him, Bhupati spends some time with Charu. Yet Charu has no misgivings even when she sees Bhupati's face. This extreme insensitivity and preoccupation shown by Charu (instances of which are absent in the first half of the story) can only suggest that her feelings for Amal are no longer limited to the straightforward affection of a sister-in-law. The truth here is that Charu's involvement is running very deep. If that is not the case it must be said that Charu's behaviour in this scene is not consistent with her behaviour described before. The scriptwriter has the right to choose the first of these two options, and that is what I did.

(c) Once he gets an idea of his sister-in-law's feelings, Amal agrees at once to get married, which proves that from his side there is no involvement and, even if there is, he is not prepared to take it any further. The first sign of maturity in his character comes through when he learns of Bhupati's misfortune and feels the need to come to his assistance. In the concluding part of the story, this new maturity may be seen as striking the dominant note in his character. It is worth noting that after he is married, Amal maintains no contact with Charu.

The major traits that emerge from these events regarding the characters of Amal and Charu—judged both individually and in relation to each other—provide the base on which the 'middle phase' of the film is built.

After the scene in the afternoon showing Manda and Amal, let us to go Charu's room at night. Bhupati arrives and mentions the marriage proposal for Amal. Charu is still cross with Amal. She says, 'That's good—just tell him, he'll certainly agree.'

Bhupati sends for Amal.

Amal: Dada, I haven't yet looked at those proofs.
Bhupati (pretending to be cross): Why not?
Amal: I was a little . . . I mean I was writing an article of my own.
Bhupati: What article?
Amal: Oh, it's nothing.
Bhupati: Go and bring it. I'd like to take a look.

In Tagore's story, Bhupati reads Amal's article and says, 'You've written very well. But why show it to me? What do I know of poetry?' In such a remark, there is a suggestion of an amusing contrast between Bhupati and Amal. That contrast is added to the scene in which they discuss marriage for Amal.

Bhupati pretends not to have understood a word of Amal's article and says, 'I say, I think you'd better get married!' Instead of raising the subject directly, he takes the opportunity to bring it up in a different way. Charu, still seething, stands behind the mosquito-net and makes various comments to provoke her brother-in-law. The two start arguing. Bhupati says, 'Why are you behaving so childishly? I haven't yet given you the most important news, Amal. When you're married, your father-in-law will send you to England.'

This is followed by temporary temptation in Amal's mind, Charu's tension, Bhupati's attempt to tempt Amal even further and, finally, Amal's refusal on the grounds that he is not really interested in going to England. (He doesn't refuse categorically. What he says is, 'Ask for more time . . . another month . . .?' He has to say that because, later in the film, he must accept the same proposal.) It is Amal's refusal that dissipates Charu's anger. I do not think that this scene distorts in any way either the theme of the novel or the nature of its characters. On the contrary, the mention of the marriage proposal in this scene prepares the ground for Amal's future acceptance and departure for England. Bearing in mind the limited confines of the film, when such an event does take place, it does not appear totally unexpected.

Immediately following this scene is a new scene involving Manda and Umapado. I have already explained why this scene was necessary. It hints at the relationship between husband and wife, as well as Umapado's villainy.

The third phase of the film starts with Amal's singing. It starts lightly enough, but leads to a second conflict between

Charu and Amal. Manda is the first person Amal informs about the publication of his article in the *Sararooha* magazine. In a fit of pique, Charu shuts the door of her room on Amal's face. Bhupati has already been involved in the friction between Charu and Amal. Now he is dragged further into the complications of the Charu–Amal–Manda relationship, which results in a complex square, filled with mixed emotions. Mr Rudra will perhaps note that in this scene, all four characters maintain their individual traits, as perceived by Tagore. Manda enjoys witnessing the battle of will between Charu and Amal, though she is slightly disappointed to find Amal trying to please Charu. Amal attempts to please both women. When Bhupati blocks his way for a moment, Amal is thrilled to inform him about the publication of his article. Bhupati asks, 'Who is going to win the election, tell me? Tory or Liberal?' Charu is still nursing her injured pride. When there is a knock on her door, she assumes it is Amal and shouts, 'I am busy!' But when she hears Bhupati's voice, she has to control herself, open the door and tell a lie to explain why she had shut it. Bhupati believes her innocently, tries to find the cockroach Charu was supposed to be looking for and, when he fails, starts to talk to her about politics.

Charu is not pacified in this scene because Amal, in keeping with his characteristic insensitivity, fails to grasp the measure of her ire. So he doesn't even try to placate her. On the contrary, he goes to Manda (as he does in the original story) and raises his voice to say, 'I'm off now to tell my friends about it!'

What follows is based very much on Tagore's original novel. 'She will write—she will amaze Amal. She won't rest until she proves that there is a great deal of difference between Manda and herself.'

In her first few attempts, Charu appears to be copying

Amal's style. In the film this is shown through the title she chooses for her essay. Amal's essays are called *The Moon in July*, *The Clouds in August*, *Light on a Moonless Night*. Charu writes *The Call of a Koel*. It is the call of that bird that makes her choose her subject on the spot. There is therefore no question here of any special inspiration. It is for this reason that no further words emerge from her pen for she does not possess Amal's easy, flowery language, or shallow emotions.

After much thought and many torn pieces of paper, Charu finally finds the source from which her writing must flow. She writes about her memories of her village. Her article is published. Charu is at last pacified—but only after she takes the magazine to Amal and strikes his head with it, hands him the slippers she had been embroidering for Bhupati, snatches the paan box from Manda to prepare a paan herself for Amal, and pulls the magazine out of Amal's hands and throws it away.

If a list is made of the various things shown in this five-minute sequence, Mr Rudra might understand something about the business of compression in a film.

(a) Charu's natural talent for writing is far greater than Amal's.

(b) Charu is not really interested in seeing her essay published. What is more important to her is to be able to prove to Amal that she is more gifted than Manda.

(c) By snatching the paan box from Manda, Charu suggests that only she (Charu) can have a claim on Amal; in the world inhabited by the two of them, no one else is allowed entry.

(d) Handing over Bhupati's embroidered slippers to Amal is the first indication of Charu straying from her wifely duties. In the original story, there are many such instances of Charu neglecting her husband.

At the end of the scene, stung by remorse, Charu breaks

down, holds Amal by his shirt and cries copiously. Then somehow she manages to pull herself together and leaves the room. Amal is seen standing by the window, still as a statue. In the story, it had dawned upon him that 'he was about to step into a gorge . . .' This scene is a reflection of that same realization. The context here is different, but there is a reason for that. In the original novel, the situation that alerts Amal to Charu's feelings is something that he has faced before, on several occasions. What must be remembered here is that Amal does not yet know the reason behind Bhupati's 'pale and stricken' looks; hence, if the revelation regarding Charu's feelings comes to Amal purely through Charu's indifference towards Bhupati, even before he has learnt the real reason behind Bhupati's crisis or its significance, such a revelation—at least in the film—may well appear to be an instance of clairvoyance.

However, the revelation is necessary for the screenplay as well. The only way to bring it about is to make Charu's behaviour more direct and obvious. That is why she has to cry in that scene. It is not an unnatural thing to do, as by then her hurt pride has been appeased and she is able to show her feelings more openly. As a matter of fact, if she can pine for Amal in front of Bhupati (chapter 8 in the novel), why shouldn't she do so in front of Amal himself, especially when we have accepted from Tagore's own words that Charu is attracted to him?

It is for this reason that I do not understand the allegation that this scene deviates from the original. What has been conveyed through action is no more than what Tagore expressed through words. For those who haven't got a copy of *Nastaneer* handy, I quote the following lines:

. . . (Charu) lay on her stomach, buried her face in her pillow and said repeatedly, 'Amal, Amal, Amal!' She felt as if a voice travelled across the seas: 'Bouthan, what is it, Bouthan?' Charu closed her moist eyes and replied, 'Amal, why did you leave in a fit of anger? I did nothing wrong, did I? If you had said goodbye properly, perhaps I would not have felt such pain.' She uttered each word exactly as she would have done if Amal was present before her: 'Amal, I haven't forgotten you, even for a day. Not one day, not one moment. All that is precious in my life was made to blossom only by you, I will worship you every day for the best part of my life!'

The scene that follows the one in which Charu breaks down gives one an idea of Bhupati's circle of friends. The original novel mentions Nishikanto more than once. This scene brings Nishikanto to life. In the same scene, Umapado is seen leaving the gathering of friends to steal money from Bhupati's safe. A few words need to be said about the changes made here to the original text.

In the novel, Umapado is caught. At least from Umapado's side, his capture does not seem unexpected. It seems as if he was *prepared* to be caught. Does that mean Umapado is a fool? But that cannot be, judging by the cunning with which he behaves. In the film, a mixture of such foolishness and deceit would not have appeared convincing. In *Nastaneer*, because of this mixture, the scene involving Bhupati and Umapado that Tagore describes at this stage does not spring to life. Umapado is turned into a totally spineless creature.

For these reasons, Umapado had to be perceived as a full-fledged calculating villain. It is natural that a character like this will cause devastating damage to Bhupati, then run away before he can be caught. It does nothing to reduce the degree of Bhupati's disillusionment (which is really the component necessary for tragedy). And because Umapado is so calculating,

Bhupati simply cannot guess what he is really like, although they work together.

The scene I am talking about here shows events taking place at night. In the friendly gathering in Bhupati's house, there is talk of current politics, then a song written by Rammohan Roy is sung (both were used to create the right period atmosphere). Umapado steals the money, Charu and Amal talk in Charu's room, there is an indication that Umapado and Manda's departure is imminent and, finally, Nishikanto draws Bhupati's attention to Charu's article which has been published in the *Vishwabandhu* magazine.

In the preceding scene, we have seen Charu snatching Amal away from Manda. So in this particular scene Manda is absent. After all, even Manda has her own pride. When they hear strains of Rammohan's song coming from the living room, Charu and Amal begin talking about England. Charu cannot help raising the subject of Amal's marriage proposal, since Amal has not expressed his views on this matter clearly enough. Amal avoids the issue. In the original, too, Amal does not agree to the proposal until it is possible for him to leave Bhupati's shelter. In order to stop their conversation from turning simply into a chat between two lovers, Amal is given the task of starting a game using alliterations with the letter 'b'. Charu has no objection to it—she, too, gets engrossed in the game because she has no inkling at this stage that she and Amal are about to be separated.

In the very next scene, Bhupati learns of Umapado's betrayal through one of their paper suppliers.

The same night, we find Amal and Charu on a veranda (it seemed eminently desirable *not* to show Charu's bedroom in this scene). Both are worried by the delay in Bhupati's return. Is it not possible that, while she fears Bhupati might be in danger, Charu is also afraid here that she might lose Amal, especially when Amal has given her no clear indication that her feelings for him are reciprocated? If we accept that Charu's feelings for Amal are not just those of a sister-in-law, but also of a lover, her reaction ought to appear quite natural.

That is why, when Amal is about to leave to look for Bhupati, Charu grabs his hand and says, 'Whatever happens, promise me you won't leave from here!' Amal replies, 'Let me go, Bouthan. I have to find out what's happened to Dada.' The loyalty that Amal shows Bhupati towards the end of the original novel is introduced in this scene. The amazement he feels at Charu's indifference towards her husband is also taken from the novel.

Bhupati tells Amal about the tragedy. This is not mentioned in *Nastaneer*. All it says is, 'Amal made enquiries and learnt about the affair.' It is important that Amal should learn the truth. But how could he be shown 'making enquiries'? By introducing new characters and new scenes? What is more objectionable: new faces and new scenes, or simply that Bhupati himself should tell Amal about the whole business? 'Bhupati could not bring himself to tell Charulata every detail of Umapado's betrayal,' says Tagore. That is natural since Umapado is Charu's brother. But is there any valid reason why Bhupati should not tell Amal everything, particularly when Amal is not wholly indifferent to Bhupati's newspaper? I don't think there is. Besides, it adds to the dramatic effect because there is a chance here to draw a wonderful parallel between Bhupati placing his trust in Umapado, as much as he places his trust in Amal. That is the line that was taken when writing the screenplay.

After his conversation with Amal, Bhupati goes to his bedroom. Charu embraces him, but cannot put on an act and offer him verbal sympathy. Bhupati misunderstands the reason behind her embrace. He tells her affectionately, 'I will now be able to spend a lot of time with you. I have got rid of your *shoteen*.' (Literally, '*shoteen*' means 'the other wife'. Since Bhupati's newspaper took up all his time, he refers to it as Charu's *shoteen*.)

Amal has now grasped the situation from Bhupati's words. He realizes the devastation Bhupati is facing. In the next scene, in keeping with the norms of cinema, Amal's action conveys the maturity that in the novel is expressed through Amal's thoughts. He writes a letter to Bhupati, leaves his house and goes off to be independent.

Bhupati finds his letter in the morning, but naturally fails to fathom the unwritten but real reason behind his departure. Charu takes out her enormous frustration first on her servant by flying into a rage quite unnecessarily, and then by making sarcastic comments about Amal ('Go and make some enquiries—you'll see that he's gone to Burdwan, nowhere else!'). Burdwan is the place from where Amal's marriage proposal had been sent.

Mr Rudra has stated that after Amal's departure, Tagore wrote another six chapters before he had Bhupati finally realizing the tragedy that had befallen him; and I dropped all of that in order to make my point as quickly as possible.

In the last six chapters of the novel, Tagore describes various subtle complexities in the Charu–Bhupati relationship. This section might be seen as focusing purely on variations on the theme of incompatibility. The compassion, the poetic qualities and the deep emotions that underline this section are undeniable. However, if one analyses the various events through which the author takes Bhupati before he reaches the final moment of truth, one is bound to spot certain weaknesses (here, again, everything boils down to the plot). I think if the film followed the original novel in toto, those weaknesses would have become glaringly obvious.

In the novel, we find Bhupati—in the early stages of this section—trying to get closer to Charu. Having lost his newspaper, he now has all the time in the world. He tries writing literature like Amal, in order to gain a place in Charu's heart. Such an attempt is most poignant. Charu, of course, finds no relief from her own pain because she cannot forget Amal. How can Bhupati fill the void left by him?

When Amal does not write from England, Charu is naturally worried. But what should be noted is that it is not as if Amal has not written at all. He writes to Bhupati, and sends his 'pronaam' (respectful greetings) to Charu—not just once, but three times. Such greetings make Charu feel as if someone has sprinkled salt on an open wound. In chapter 18, Tagore says:

> Although Amal did tell Bhupati that he would be too busy with his studies to write frequently, when one or two mail deliveries passed without any letter from him, Charu's entire world turned sour. In the evening, having spoken of various other things, she asked her husband, calmly and casually, 'Look, why don't we send a telegram to Amal in England and find out how he is?' Bhupati replied, 'I had a letter from him two weeks ago. He is very busy with his studies.'

If that is the case, what does Charu hope to gain by sending Amal a prepaid telegram? She knows why he is busy. From his letter to Bhupati, she has learnt that Amal is well. Does she hope that, in his reply to the prepaid telegram, Amal will say something to suggest that he is still attracted to her? But he got married and went to England at Bhupati's request, thereby showing clearly that he wanted to put an end to his relationship with Charu.

Let us now examine the actual despatch of the telegram.
It cannot be sent in Bhupati's presence, in case he gets suspicious.
Charu therefore has to resort to deception. One or two days
after her conversation with Bhupati, she tells him, 'My sister
is now in Chuchro. Can you go there today and find out how
she is?'

> Bhupati: Why, is she ill?
> Charu: No, she isn't ill. But you know how pleased they all feel
>   to see you!
> At Charu's request, Bhupati got into his carriage and began his
> journey to Howrah station. On his way there, the road was
> blocked at one point by a row of bullock carts. While he waited,
> a postman he knew who distributed telegrams turned up and
> handed him a telegram.

An analysis here is unnecessary. Even Mr Rudra will realize—
if he thinks a little about it—that not even a tiny portion of
the above event would have appeared convincing in a film.

When he learns about Charu's telegram, 'a vague suspicion—
almost unconsciously—began to sting him (Bhupati)'.

How does this suspicion take firm root?

> Charu could hardly make herself stand still. All her work was
> neglected, she made mistakes in whatever she did, her servants
> began stealing, people noticed her shabby looks and began
> whispering, nothing brought Charu to her senses. Gradually, it
> came to a stage when Charu would start for no reason, get up
> and leave in the middle of a conversation just to shed tears, turn
> pale if she so much as heard Amal's name. In the end, even
> Bhupati saw it all, and the thought that had not occurred to him
> for a moment now stared him in the face. The world, to him,
> became old, dry and worn out.

In this portion of the story, when there is no question of
Bhupati being absorbed in his work, when he is eager to spend
his time with Charu and when Charu's feelings are so obvious
that 'people' begin to whisper, where does one find the
psychological basis for this marathon incomprehension on
Bhupati's part? He had knowingly neglected Charu; the novel
even bears hints of his feeling of guilt; he is conscious of the
basic incompatibility between Charu and himself. Moreover,
he has received—more than once—indications of Charu's
tenderness and affection towards Amal. Tagore did *not*
imagine Bhupati to be a complete idiot. I have said this before,
and I will say it again: when one reads the novel, the sheer beauty
and power of Tagore's language wipe out these inconsistencies.
But when writing a screenplay, one has to make a ruthless
analysis of the original story, imagine the characters as people
of flesh and blood, bring to life the atmosphere described in
the story, and arrange the scattered events in such a way that
a chronological thread may then bind them together. When
one is doing this, one cannot help having doubts and noticing
flaws. If the original story is changed at times, it is for this
reason—not because one has had a sudden whim, or one wants
to make a film from someone else's story, and clamour for
credit by claiming to have created something totally original.
Mr Rudra may well ask: then why choose a story like *Nastaneer*?
In reply, I shall say: simply to make a film like *Charulata*.

I shall end this discussion with an analysis of whether or
not the epilogue of *Charulata* is completely different from
the epilogue of *Nastaneer*.

In Tagore's story, after Amal's departure, the main aim
behind Bhupati's behaviour is to try to get closer to Charu.
This is spread over a period of time. In the film, the scene shifts
from the city to hint at this passage of time. Husband and

wife are seen on a beach, faraway from their normal surroundings. Has Charu been able to forget Amal? There is no indication of that in this scene. Bhupati's presence prevents any such indication. Besides, if Charu *appears* here to have forgotten Amal, the scene that follows, revealing the truth about her failure to do so, becomes more heartrending. On the beach, therefore, there is no mention of Amal.

Although Charu speaks normally with Bhupati, she makes no comment on his attempt to sound romantic. On the contrary, by picking out a grey strand from Bhupati's hair she makes a somewhat unromantic gesture. However, as in the original novel, Charu is never harsh or aggressive while conversing with Bhupati; in this particular scene, too, she is most encouraging when the subject of Bhupati restarting his newspaper comes up.

Only a few minutes after their return to Calcutta, Bhupati hands Charu a letter from Amal. As soon as he steps out of the room—without even opening Amal's letter—Charu breaks down under the weight of her pent-up pain and anguish. Bhupati returns unexpectedly, and stops at the threshold on seeing his wife crying her heart out. He can also hear her lament: 'Thakurpo (term used for Amal, meaning brother-in-law), why did you have to go, Thakurpo? What was my crime, what did I do that you had to leave without a word to me . . .?'

In the film, Bhupati has never been shown as being such an idiot that he should now mistake Charu's words as those coming from a woman who feels nothing but normal ties of affection with her brother-in-law. Even so, in order for him to grasp the situation fully, he is shown being driven alone in a horse-drawn carriage for a long time. Different emotions play on his face—there is disbelief, pain, dejection and, finally, pity for Charu.

Bhupati returns home.

In a story set in the nineteenth century, there is no question of a divorce. So will Bhupati go elsewhere, leaving Charu on her own, as he does in *Nastaneer*? Is Charu's 'crime' completely unpardonable in Bhupati's eyes, or does he believe that Charu will suffer relatively less pain if she is left alone? Isn't Bhupati also likely to feel an urge to have a major showdown with his wife? Especially when he himself is responsible, to a considerable degree, for the whole situation?

In my view, abandoning Charu and leaving for Mysore is not in keeping with the character of Bhupati, as described by Tagore.

But is it possible to build a new happy home under the prevailing circumstances? Is it possible for the two to be united? Is it possible for them to forgive each other and live together again?

Whatever happens and whatever is possible, the situation will certainly take time to resolve. Bhupati and Charu now know each other rather too well; so the gulf between them seems unbridgeable.

In the final scene, therefore, the two hands cannot meet. Might they meet in the future? One doesn't know; nor is there any need to know. Tagore himself felt no need to find an unequivocal answer. For the moment, Charu and Bhupati's home is broken, their trust is shattered, and both have had to leave their world of childish make-believe and face the harsh realities of life. That is the most important thing to remember. That is the theme of *Nastaneer*.

In my view, that theme remains perfectly intact in *Charulata*.

14

Alias Indir Thakrun

I can never forget the state of my mind on the day I first
went to see Chunibala Devi in her house in Paikpara. The
film (*Pather Panchali*) was already underway. Cast had been
finalized for the roles of Apu, Durga, Harihar and Sarbajaya.
I had also decided who I'd use for Prasanna, Shejo Thakrun
and Nilmoni's wife. The only major character left was Indir
Thakrun.

'She was an old woman of seventy-five, her cheeks were
sunken, her back was slightly bent and her body leant forward;
things in the distance were no longer easily visible to her'—it
was not easy to find an actress to fit the description given by
Bibhuti Bhushan, especially when our advertisement in the
press had announced time and again: 'no make-up is going to
be used in this film.' It was not as if we had not tried to look
for an old woman who fitted the description, but her
appearance was not the only thing we had to worry about.
The biggest worry was whether an old lady well into her
seventies would be able to withstand the exertions of outdoor
shooting. Besides, age could often affect one's mental prowess
in varying degrees. Could Indir's memory be trusted? In other
words, could she memorize her lines and speak them in front

'Orofe Indir Thakrun', *Madhyabitto*, Puja Issue, 1955.

of the camera? The actress we were looking for had to be sufficiently old, able to act, put up with physical exertions and possess a brain still alert and agile. It terrifies me now to think that when we began our film, we did so without even considering whether it would be possible at all to find someone with all those four qualities.

It was Reba Devi (who played Shejo Thakrun in *Pather Panchali*) who told us about Chunibala. Chunibala was said to be Nibhanoni Devi's mother. She had worked in two silent films and, before that, had been in the theatre during the time of such actresses as Tarasundari and Nagendrabala. We collected Nibhanoni's address and turned up at her house on a Sunday morning.

Chunibala did not disappoint us. 'An old woman of seventy-five, her cheeks were sunken, her back slightly bent and her body leant forward . . .' She fitted the description quite satisfactorily.

'Do you know any rhymes? Can you recite poetry?' I asked.

Chunibala recited a nursery rhyme for us: *Ghoom parani maashi pishi* (*Come to our house, Auntie Lullaby*). I had always heard ten or twelve lines of it—that was all I thought there was. The rhyme that emerged through Chunibala's lips was surprisingly longer. It could be that what she recited was the original and authentic version. I had to admire the memory of this old lady. Most of my fears were removed. Now I asked her the second important question.

'You will have to leave here at six in the morning, travel to a village fifteen miles from here and spend the whole day shooting. Then in the evening, you will be driven back home. Do you think you can manage that?'

'*Certainly!*'

This time, all my fears were put to rest.

While working with Chunibala Devi, I kept thinking just one thing: if we hadn't found her, *Pather Panchali* would never have been made. She grasped, right from the start, that we were not going in for anything fake or artificial. 'Since you have chosen *me* instead of a young actress simply made up to look like an old woman, I can see what you're really interested in doing,' she said to me, and made sure that at least her own portrayal of Indir remained realistic throughout.

Let me give an example. Chunibala was given a plain old white cotton sari to wear to show that she was a widow. The sari was torn in many places. 'Indir was known to tie knots to cover the tears. You can tie as many knots as you like, it's up to you,' I told her. After a few days of shooting, the old sari became much more threadbare. One day, I overheard Chunibala muttering, 'This sari is so badly torn now, I can hardly cover myself properly!' The next day, she was given another sari with fewer tears. Chunibala said nothing. When she appeared for shooting, dressed as Indir, we saw that she had rejected the new sari and was still wearing the old one.

I have already mentioned her memory. The way she could remember small details to help with continuity was really amazing. There might well have been mistakes in our files, but not in her mind. 'Look, my right hand was wet, wasn't it, when you took the previous shot the other day?'; 'Why, you haven't put any perspiration on my face!'; 'I'm not supposed to wear a shawl in this shot!'; 'Was I carrying this bundle in my right hand before? No, it was in my left hand. I had the pot in my right!' She frequently made such remarks.

Among Chunibala's many talents was her ability to sing. We discovered it much later. One day, at the end of our shooting, we were all having tea in the evening on the little veranda attached to Harihar's house. 'Can you sing?' I asked Chunibala.

In the novel—or in the original screenplay—there was no mention of Indir singing. But, over a period of time, I had started to think that it might not be a bad idea to show Indir singing during an idle moment. There would only be her voice, no other accompaniment.

'Will a religious song do?' she asked.

'Yes,' I replied.

Indir sang:

Say 'Hari', my heart,
and cross the ocean of life.
Hari is in the water, on land,
on the moon and the sun—
His presence fills the universe.

The song was recorded.

Only a few days later, we ran out of money and work on the film came to a halt.

Almost a year later, I finally got the chance to shoot Indir's song when we were working in a studio, shooting some night scenes. Indir was going to be shown sitting on the western side of the veranda on a moonlit night. She would be singing quietly to herself, her legs outstretched, keeping time with one hand. In the background there would be croaking frogs and chirping crickets. The camera would slowly get closer to her.

A few minutes before we were to take the shot, Chunibala said, 'I have remembered another song. It's even better. Do you want to hear it?'

Hari, the day is over, it's dusk,
ferry me across.
I have heard that you are the master

who takes people across.
So I pray to you.
I hear you help even those
who do not have a penny.
I am poor, like a beggar.
Look, in my bag,
There's not a single penny.
Hari, the day is over, it's dusk,
ferry me across.

The script of *Pather Panchali* sometimes deviated from the events described in the novel. Chunibala raised no objection to anything, except the scene which shows Indir's death. She said, 'The novel shows her dying near a temple. Indir was a most religious old woman . . . is it fair to show her dying in a bamboo grove?' I tried explaining to her that if the two children discovered her corpse in a bamboo grove purely by chance, the emotions that discovery might arouse in their young minds would be most significant, both from the point of view of cinema, and in creating a dramatic effect. Chunibala said nothing more.

The scene in question shows Durga spotting her in the wood. Indir happens to be sitting with her head pressed between her knees. Durga thinks she is asleep, and shakes her by her shoulder. Indir's body remains in a sitting position for a few seconds before losing its balance and falling to the ground with a thud. Needless to say, the responsibility for making this scene realistic rested solely on Chunibala. Her acting—and the shot—could be deemed successful only if she could throw her body straight to the ground without worrying about sustaining serious injuries. The film bears full evidence of how well Chunibala passed this difficult test. And I shall always remember the expression on her face when the shot was over, reflecting a mixture of her mental satisfaction and physical pain.

Before I end this essay, I must cite one more incident, also related to Indir's death.

The scene of her funeral procession was shot when most of the work on the film was already finished. This scene was not in the original screenplay, either. It was added later, on the grounds that it might make Indir's death even more poignant. Some people think that the very sight of a dead body on its final journey is horrible. I do not think so. In my view, there are two reasons why Indir's journey does not appear horrible in the film. One, the natural surroundings and the time (soon after sunrise) at which the shot was taken. Two, the absence of the usual chants of 'Bolo Hari!' and 'Haribol!'

I know from experience that there are always some people in the audience who cannot resist the temptation of saying 'Haribol!' if they hear 'Bolo Hari!' It was with these people in mind that the decision *not* to use such chants was made. The decision to use the old lady's song as background music came as a natural progression.

Chunibala Devi arrived in a taxi at five a.m. and found us waiting by a track that ran through a field, getting ready for the shot. She had no idea what the scene involved and why she had been brought there. Somehow I managed to muster enough courage to say to her, 'Today we'll put you up on a bier!' Chunibala was not in the least taken aback or put out. 'Very well. How many people can experience such a thing? I have no objection at all!' she said.

We spread a mat over a cot made of bamboo and asked Indir to lie on it. Then her body was wrapped tightly with the shawl that she had begged from her nephew, Raju. Ropes were then tied across the bier to make it more secure. This was followed by a rehearsal for the benefit of the camera, and the funeral procession started.

When the shot was over, the bier was lowered to the ground, the ropes untied. But Chunibala did not move. We exchanged glances. What was the matter with her? My heart gave a sudden lurch.

In the next instant, however, I heard Chunibala's voice: 'Has the shot been taken already? Why, nobody told *me*! So I was still pretending to be a corpse!'

Her acting was truly extraordinary. With that shot, Indir's role came to an end.

15

Two Characters

When I left my job in advertising and stepped into film-making, the chief attraction that cinema held for me was simply to do with its art. Of course, there was also the hope that, through that art, I might find permanent employment. What I couldn't possibly have known in the beginning was that film-making might offer something in addition to the sheer joy one could derive from the job, or the remuneration that went with it.

Today, I am aware that while a film is being made, one might have experiences that would make a lasting impression, even though they might not be directly related to the film. So far, I have made ten films. It is really difficult to recall every detail of our daily activities while those films were being made. What stand out in my memory instead—with amazing clarity—are some incidents and a few characters who appeared during their making. Two such characters were Subodh-da of the village called Boral, and Mr Ramani Ranjan Sen of Varanasi.

Boral was chosen to shoot *Pather Panchali*. On a cold winter morning, as we were going down a village path with all our paraphernalia to find the right spot, a voice suddenly reached our ears. 'The film company is here! Grab your spears and jump, all of you. Grab your spears and jump!' it said.

'Dui Charitra', *Desh*, Puja Issue, 1962.

Investigations revealed that the man who had spoken was called Subodh-da. For the last ten years, he had been mentally disturbed. He did not trust anyone. Most certainly he would not trust a film unit. Strangely, though, we got to know Subodh-da in due course. In fact, he became quite close to us. Whenever there was a free moment, I would go and sit on the little balcony in front of his house; and, immediately, he would bring out a dusty old gunny bag. Then he would take out a number of ancient legal documents from it and rattle off a list to prove how much land he owned, and how various people were cheating him. According to Subodh-da, each of his fellow villagers had fraud and deceit in his blood. One day, he said, 'Suppose, on a moonless night, ten people are walking down a path in single file. None of them has a light—they are so tight-fisted, see? The first man slips and falls into a pothole, but picks himself up and continues walking. He does nothing to warn the man behind him. So, one by one, each of those ten men falls into the same hole, but no one speaks up, lest it helps the others. That's how the people of Boral are!'

Subodh-da referred to very few people by their real names. 'See that man on a bicycle? You know who he is? Roosevelt. You'll need to watch him very carefully—he's a crook!'

Roosevelt, Churchill, Fazlul Huq, Alibardi Khan, Hitler . . . they were all Subodh-da's neighbours, all of them had to be avoided.

One day, I said to Subodh-da, 'I believe you can play the violin? Why, you have never played for us!'

At once, he disappeared inside and returned with a case containing his violin. 'What would you like to hear? Iman or Bagesree?' he asked.

'Let's have Iman,' I replied.

'Sa-pa-pa-ppa-ma-ga-ma-ni-dha-ni!' Subodh-da hummed the first tune to himself before applying his bow to the violin.

Over the next half an hour, he played various tunes, all set in Iman. Then he stopped. His hand was clearly not as steady as it must have been once, but there was no doubt that he understood music.

Subodh-da described to us one day how his madness started. 'There I was, sitting quietly, when suddenly my eyes were dazzled. It was as if I'd seen a divine spark. And then I saw her. Ma Jagadamba, the goddess. She had torn herself free—shackles and all—and was flying towards the sky. She was wearing a striped sari, her hair flowed down to her waist, and on her feet were canvas shoes. Bas, my head began to reel and . . . that's all it took!'

Nearly five years later, I went to Boral on some work. I stopped outside Subodh-da's house and called out his name. He came out at once. There was a subtle difference in his appearance. He wore a relaxed, detached air and looked a little listless. The gunny bag was missing, and so were his eternal complaints against his fellow beings. We sat on the balcony for a while. Then he said, 'Why didn't you come during the mango season, my friend? We had very good mangoes this year.'

He did not say anything much after this. On my way back, I learned from other villagers that about six months ago, Subodh-da's mental problems had been cured, entirely on their own.

***

I first met Mr Ramani Ranjan Sen on a ghat in Varanasi. It was the winter of 1957. We were looking for suitable cast for *Aparajito*. One of the characters in the film was Bhavataran

Chatterjee, Sarbajaya's uncle. An old man was required to play him. I wanted to use an amateur actor, if I could; failing that, I would use someone who was not an actor at all.

One evening, I found Ramani Ranjan in the crowd gathered to listen to kirtan on Dashashwamedh Ghat. His looks were very close to those I had imagined Bhavataran to possess. On that first day, however, I failed to find the courage to talk to him. Who knew what might happen if, out of the blue, I went and asked an old man in his seventies to act in a film? But when I saw him again, I *had* to muster all my courage and approach him. The kirtan was about to begin; within a few seconds, the drummer would start playing. Reproduced below, word for word, is the conversation I had with the old man on the second day:

> I: Namaskar! Please don't mind my talking to you like this. I . . . I mean, I am . . . a director. A film director. Films . . . er . . . I mean I make bioscopes. I am currently working on a film based on Bibhuti Bhushan's novel, *Aparajito*. In that novel, there is a character who is an old man and he lives in Varanasi. It's a very good role. Excellent. So . . . the thing is, you see, a film doesn't always have to use professional actors. So, I was wondering . . . if . . . what if *you* were to do that role?
>
> Old Man: *Koroom na kyan*? (Why shouldn't I?)

That was all.

I could find no answer for his '*koroom na kyan*?', nor did I find it necessary even to look for an answer. When I thought about it later, it did occur to me that the old man could easily have found a thousand different reasons for *not* taking up my offer. That he agreed was a most unexpected deviation from what would have been normal behaviour for him.

Even now, it is not clear to me why Ramani Ranjan agreed

to complicate his simple and peaceful life by getting into the complex business of acting in a film (payment could not have been a consideration—that came much later). What was even more surprising was that the old man had never seen a film in his life, nor acted in amateur theatre.

It is sometimes quite difficult to get a good performance from an actor. Working with Ramani Ranjan was relatively easy. I never saw him get nervous and stiff, or be camera-shy. On the contrary, he showed concern for his fellow actors. One day, we were getting ready to shoot a scene on Sarbajaya's veranda. It would show Apu (Pinaki Sengupta) and Bhavataran having their dinner. Sarbajaya would sit nearby, fanning them. Bhavataran would speak his lines, immediately after which Apu would pick up his glass of water and take a sip from it. The rehearsal went without a hitch. We got ready to take the shot. Everything was in place. The camera started, the two actors began eating, the fan in Sarbajaya's hand swung into motion. Bhavataran took his cue and spoke his lines. But, as soon as he finished speaking, he lifted his left index finger and jabbed Apu's waist with it.

I could only gape. Quickly, I switched the camera off and said, 'Dadu, why on earth did you do that? Why did you jab him with your finger?'

Dadu replied, '*Or jol khaaoner kotha na eikhane? Polapaan, jodi bhuila jai?*' (Wasn't he supposed to drink water at that point? He's only a young boy, suppose he forgot?)

He was so anxious about other people's acting; but about his own he seemed completely relaxed. I have never seen even a professional actor remain so perfectly unruffled.

Ramani Ranjan retained an active interest in the future of *Aparajito*. When we finished shooting in Varanasi and returned to Calcutta, he kept sending us postcards from time to time:

'Kindly oblige me by letting me know how far you have got in completing your *paala*.' He did not ever refer to a film as anything other than a 'paala', a word that was once used for folk theatre.

On the last day of his shooting, Ramani Ranjan had some really difficult lines to speak. They were difficult because they could not be rattled off one after the other. What they had to convey were disjointed thoughts, and unless there were suitable gaps in the right places, the whole effect would be ruined. The scene showed a few days after Sarbajaya's death. Apu was sitting on their balcony, crying, his head pressed between his knees. Bhavataran was seated on the opposite corner, leaning against a pole and smoking a hookah, while trying to comfort his niece's son. 'Don't cry, Apu, please don't. Parents can't live for ever, can they? I think you should stay here with me, and start working as a priest again. What's the point in studying any further? Much better if you stayed here.'

We did not have to use more than one take. Ramani Ranjan spoke those lines in between inhaling from his hookah, and every word came out with amazing spontaneity. When we packed up for the day, I went to the old man and said most gratefully, 'Dadu, your performance today was really good!'

I can still hear Dadu's reply. He frowned slightly and said in a grave voice, without even turning towards me: '*Boli, kharap da hoilo kaube*?' (I say, when was it ever bad?)

16

Benode-da

I did not know Benode Bihari Mukhopadhyay—either by name or through his work—before 1940, probably because I had not noticed any pictures drawn by him in the pages of the *Probashi* magazine.

My mother had often expressed the wish that I should spend some time in Santiniketan after finishing college. I myself was hopeful of pursuing a career in art, perhaps commercial art. Santiniketan did not teach commercial art; the art they taught was Oriental. At the time, Oriental Art meant only one thing to me: the colour picture on the first page of *Probashi*. With the exception of Nandalal Bose, no artist produced anything in the standard tricolour halftone art plates that seemed worthy of attention. The business of wash-painting struck me as wishy-washy; and my mind always rebelled against the suggestion of a soft sentimentality in both the subject matter and style adopted in those paintings. Anyway, eventually I turned up at Kala Bhavan, in the belief that in order to study commercial art in this country, I ought to know something of the ancient traditions of Indian art.

The first person whose work I noticed within five minutes of my arrival at the ashram was Benode Bihari Mukhopadhyay.

'Benode-da', *Desh Binodan*, 1971.

Arrangements had been made for me to stay in a new three-room hostel in Kala Bhavan. I had to climb three steps to get to the front veranda. As soon as I did, my eyes went automatically to the ceiling. It was covered with a mural. What it depicted was a rural scene, complete with trees, meadows, lakes, people, birds and animals—gentle yet glowing with colour. It was a village in Birbhum. Perhaps it would be better to call it a tapestry rather than a mural. Or an encyclopaedia. It was a painting of such calibre that none of the definitions of Oriental Art that had once poisoned my mind could be applied to it.

I spent the next two-and-a-half years in Santiniketan and, in that time, got the chance to learn more closely about Benode Bihari's art and his views. Gradually, what became clear was his isolation in the world of art and artists. Seen against modern Indian art, his single-minded dedication, his sound knowledge about the rules and methods applied to art, as well as the desire to learn more, seemed amazing to me.

On visiting the Poush mela in January 1950, I was able to see Benode-da's latest work of art. Three sides of a wall in Hindi Bhavan were covered by murals showing the lives of Indian saints and sages in the middle ages. I do not know of any work of art in our country created this century that is more noble or more successful. If there is any real connoisseur of art who is not familiar with Benode Bihari's work, I would urge him to visit Santiniketan at once and see that mural.

It is not my intention here to make an evaluation of Benode Bihari's art. I happened to talk to him recently on various matters while making a documentary on him. I wish to present before the readers certain portions of that conversation. Those unfamiliar with the world of art might not know that for the last fifteen years, Benode Bihari has been totally blind. He was born partially blind, in any case. One of his eyes did not work at all, the other was extremely weak. He wore thick lenses and had to peer at a canvas from only a few inches away in order to look at or draw a picture. He works even now at Kala Bhavan as one of its teachers. His very simple home is nearby. Although he cannot see, he has planned a mural recently. He spends a couple of hours every morning working on it. The afternoon is his time to rest. That is when he sits on a wicker chair in his living room. His eyes are hidden behind dark glasses; in front of him—on a cane table—are kept his cigarettes, matches and ashtray. On the floor, between his feet, stands a waste paper basket containing a flask of black tea placed at an angle. He spoke to me during an afternoon, pausing every now and then to smoke and to drink his tea.

'I was born in Behala in my mother's home, in 1903. My ancestral home is in Garalgachha. Your film actor Sailen's [who played Bhupati in *Charulata*] father, Indu Mukherjee, was my first cousin. I lived in Calcutta until I was thirteen. North Calcutta. Are those alleyways still the same, or have they changed? Is that statue of Keshtodas Pal still there? Painting exhibitions used to be held under that statue. Small oil paintings. Landscapes. Made by a Bengali painter. I used to go to look at them with my elder brother, Bijanbihari. We got to know the painter. He was a nice man, and quite independent-minded. He used to say: "This is a sort of experiment, this exhibition. Let's see how people respond." My brother was most enthusiastic about drawing. Once he asked that artist about the use of a palette-knife. The gentleman said: "I don't know anything about that. I am just an ordinary artist, I don't understand such technicalities."

'Our family was free of religious orthodoxy, influenced to some extent by Brahmoism. My mother followed all the rituals in her daily worship, but there was never any rigidity about anything. My only sister—older than me—became a widow, but she was remarried. Hers was the fourth case of widow remarriage in Bengal. Virtually everyone in my family could draw, it was inborn in all of us. I was the youngest of six brothers. You have heard the name of my second brother, Bonobihari, haven't you? He was a well-known cartoonist in those days. His drawings were published in the *Bharatvarsh* magazine. And *Shonibarer Chithi*. He had many other talents, too. Not many people know about it. He had a major influence on me.

'I remember very well three paintings that I saw in my childhood. They used to hang on a wall in our house. Two were mythological, the artist was Bamapodo Bandopadhyay. One had the title *Kalanka Bhanjan* and the other was *Durbashaar Abhishaap*. The third was a Western painting, its title was *Absence Makes the Heart Grow Fonder*. At the time I knew nothing about Indian art. I merely looked at drawings and paintings, and liked some of them—paintings by Abanindranath, Subodh Ganguli, Sukhalata Rao, Upendrakishore Ray. People used to gather outside Upendrakishore's house in Sukea Street. Inside the house there would be singing—chorus—and someone would play the violin. People gathered to hear all that music.

'Baba bought Bijanbihari a notebook. He made a lot of sketches of the city of Calcutta in it. It was my favourite notebook. I wanted to bring it with me to Santiniketan, but people told me not to. They said, all those sketches used a Western style, they would not be suitable for Santiniketan. Remember that saying—you can't learn Indian art if you wear a twill shirt? This was something similar!

'Santidev's father, Kalimohan Ghosh, was responsible for

my coming to Santiniketan. He knew my brother. He said, "Send this brother of yours to Gurudev's ashram." By then I had been to three or four different schools. Sanskrit Collegiate School, Modern Institution and Brahmo Boys' School; my studies weren't really getting very far because of my eyes. I had a lot of treatment but even the good eye did not improve. Dr Shashi Sen said, "If he wants to learn to paint, let him do it. It's best if he doesn't try to do a lot of different things." So I finally arrived here in Santiniketan. Kalimohan took me to meet Gurudev. He had already been told about my eyesight. When we reached *Dehli* [name of building], Kalimohan said, "Take your shoes off and go in." I went in. Rabindranath looked at me and asked, "Have you had any treatment for your eyes? And it didn't work?" I shook my head. Then he said, "You do know that here in our ashram everyone has to do their own work? Will you be able to manage?" I said yes. So he said, "All right, you may go, let me speak to Kalimohan." I was afraid he might reject me outright. But that didn't happen.

'Because of my poor eyesight, I was excused from one particular duty. I didn't have to sweep the floor. When Jagadananda Roy heard about it, he asked, if he can draw, why can't he sweep the floor? I drew pictures of insects for a book by the same Jagadananda Roy. That was my first job as an artist.'

'Those who dabbled in Indian art in those days had a tendency to draw mythological scenes. Did you ever draw anything like that?' I asked Benode-da.

'No, never. I had no interest in mythology. The atmosphere in our house was responsible for that. No one seemed to care for that kind of thing. When I was a child, I remember someone in our house reading aloud from Rabindranath's *Gora*, and everyone else listening to it. So you can imagine!'

***

'I have never seen any of your films. I saw Chaplin in my young days—I remember enjoying it a great deal. Do people still see Chaplin's films?'

'Yes, they are being shown again and people are enjoying them once more.'

'Oh good. Chaplin is excellent. I have read reviews of your films, and people have come and told me about them. I remember hearing something about *Apur Sansar*. Someone came and said, "It's a good film but Satyajit Ray has made a terrible blunder in one scene." How come? So he said, "Apu's brother-in-law arrives to tell him that Apu's wife died at childbirth, and Apu—without any rhyme or reason—gives him a tight slap!" When I heard that, the whole thing struck me as extraordinary. The thing is, you see, most people either do not wish to admit the deeper truth, or do not understand it at all. Did you hear of this woman who lost many of her relatives, one after the other? In the end, when she heard about the death of one of her own children, she said: "Oh hell, how *much* can I cry?" Could you show such a thing in a film? Perhaps not. It would start a controversy.

'I think there are many things ordinary people understand far better than artists or critics just by using their common sense. There was a time when we used to sit outside in Santiniketan and paint. Local Santhals used to stand around and watch us. Once, I remember, I had drawn a herd of buffaloes. A group of Santhal women turned up. One of them saw my sketch and said, "You've drawn so many buffaloes, and you didn't think of adding a calf?" Just that one remark pointed out to me a major flaw in the picture. Nowadays no Santhal comes to look at our pictures. Even they have changed. They've left their farms and are now working in factories, which has changed their outlook. It is no longer possible to produce the kind of primitive art we've seen. There are now a lot of obstacles between having feelings and expressing them. That was not a problem before. If a primitive artist wanted to draw, a technique occurred to him naturally. Today, one has to work hard to learn techniques, and acquire a measure of sophistication. But look at the horse drawn in Altamira. A caveman, by today's standards, could hardly be called sophisticated. But those savages drew horses on stone surfaces with such style that would put a China horse to shame. That natural instinct in man is gradually disappearing.'

***

'Has any film shown blindness?' Benode-da asked.

'Oh yes, even Bengali films. Rabindranath's *Drishtidaan* was once made into a film. In the West, a film was made from Andre Zide's novel *La Symphonie Pastorale*. I remember it.'

'How is blindness portrayed? Is it realistic?'

'Blindness gets the same kind of treatment as muteness. It is shown as gently as possible, especially if the heroine herself is blind or mute. I do not remember seeing in any film the groaning noises mute people make when they try unsuccessfully to express themselves.'

'In that case, perhaps they simplify everything for blind people as well. The whole thing is actually quite complex. It wasn't possible to learn that before. What happens is that one develops a totally new concept of space. Space becomes a solid object, which has to be manually pushed aside in order to move forward. Nothing has any existence except what one can touch. You can see a chair and know that it is there; I will know that there is a chair only when I sit in it. Even then, I won't know whether or not it has arms until my hand brushes against them.

After that, it is only by touching and feeling those arms that I can tell whether they are made of wood or cane, whether they are thin or thick, smoothly polished or rough surfaced, and whether they have gone down at right angles, or are rounded in shape. I give a start if I touch something unexpectedly. I am sitting in a chair right now, and my stick is placed in front of me, diagonally across the arms of the chair. If I forget where the stick is kept and touch it accidentally, I'll jump out of my skin. There is another side to it, you see. I picked up that glass full of tea. Until I became blind, I was never really aware of how glass felt to the touch. One develops tactile feelings about every object.'

'You still sketch, don't you?'

'No, I've virtually stopped. I used to, in the beginning. Prithwish got me a few Flowmaster pens. But I've had problems. I cannot tell when I've run out of ink. I may be sketching happily, when somebody says suddenly: why, your pen's not leaving any mark on your paper! So now I've stopped. I've even begun to lose my interest in colours. I used to cut pieces of coloured paper and make collages, but now I've come to realize that it's impossible to verbally describe the exact shade of a colour. I've tried to explain it by saying it's blue like such-and-such an object, or it's as red as such-and-such a flower, but there is always a doubt about its precision. What still interests me is form. And tension. The mural I am working on now shows human figures standing next to one another—there is tension there, between those figures and in the entire composition. That's the main thing.'

'We are back to ordinary people!'

'Yes. It's all to do with things I have seen and known. You've seen it yourself—a chanachur-wala, a man carrying a pole across his shoulders, a woman with a basket on her head, a

Vaishnav couple—simple, ordinary people I have seen before. I have no interest in mechanical abstractions. That mural will grace the outside of a building, people will pass it by, at least they will be able to see that those are human figures.'

***

'You will show *khoaai** in your film, won't you?'

'I certainly wanted to—but all the *khoaai* seems to have vanished.'

'There is one place where it still exists. Taltorh. Near Prantik station. And you'll find some more if you go towards Cheep Sahib's bungalow. Don't leave the *khoaai* out. A stretch of *khoaai*, and in the middle of it, a solitary palm tree. That's all. If you wish to look for my spirit, the basic essence of all that my life stands for, you will find it there. You could say, I am *it*!'

---

*Dry, eroded earth found in Birbhum, around Santiniketan.

17

Stray Thoughts

When I think of or plan a new film, very often I find myself thinking of things related to my old films. Most of these stray thoughts concern the actors. Professionals, amateurs, half-amateurs, half-professionals, or totally new and inexperienced—there have been actors from every category. Naturally, the events that involve famous professional actors are different from those involving non-professionals. In most cases, these events are not all that significant; or what I remember may not even merit being called an 'event'. Nevertheless, I will relate a few experiences, in the belief that if they have lingered in my mind, there must be something special about them.

There are some actors with whom I did not get the chance to work more than once. This caused me the biggest regret in the case of Chunibala Devi. I came across, quite accidentally, a short story by Bibhuti Bhushan while I was still working on *Pather Panchali*. It was called *Drobomoyeer Kashibash* (Drobomoyee's Pilgrimage). I informed Chunibala the very next day that she would be given another role as soon as she finished playing Indir Thakrun. Chunibala grew very excited when she heard the story of Drobomoyee. But I never got a

---

'A-katha, Shay-katha', *Desh Binodan*, 1970.

second chance to work with her. Chunibala broke her hip and became bedridden only a short while before *Pather Panchali* was released. She did not regain the strength to resume work and remained confined to bed until she died. Drobomoyee's story could not leave the pages of a book. Is there any actress in our country who can fill the void left by Chunibala? I don't think so.

The man who was cast in the role of the headmaster in a village school in *Aparajito* had never done any acting, but had been associated with films for a long time. Subodh Ganguli had worked in his youth as an operator in various cinemas, handling the machines used to run the films. Later, he learnt to work in a laboratory and eventually became the director of the chemical laboratory owned by New Theatres. A special feature of the films produced by New Theatres in its heyday was neat and sleek photography. There is no doubt that Subodh Ganguli deserved some of the credit for it. After leaving New Theatres, he joined Aurora Company. I met him in the office of this company. His appearance, and his old-fashioned clothes (they followed a style popular in the nineteenth century), made me offer him the role of Apu's headmaster. He gave me a beaming smile and agreed at once. 'Is it a comic role?' he asked. 'I have often looked into the mirror and imagined myself to be Charlie Chaplin!'

Usually, when facing a camera, actors concern themselves only with their own performance. They do not worry about how a scene is to be shot, where the camera is being placed, or where the light is coming from; nor are they supposed to bother about such things. But Subodh Ganguli knew the technicalities of film-making so well that he couldn't help noticing these details. I would be standing before him, notebook in hand, explaining the next shot to be taken in a few moments, when

Subodh Ganguli would interrupt me and address the cameraman directly, 'Subrata babu, is the reflector falling on my face as it should? Could you please check the lights? Perhaps if it could lean to one side, it would . . .?'

Another small role in *Aparajito* went to a middle-aged actor called Kali Bandopadhyay. I first saw him in the film *Kavi* made by Devaki Basu. He played a Bihari chowkidar at a railway station. He was a comedian, and lived somewhere near the temple in Kalighat. He looked like a traditional Hindu priest, and it was a priest that I wanted him to play in my film. So there was no mistake in casting him in that role, purely from the point of view of his appearance. He went to Varanasi with us for the shooting. We stayed in a friend's house, close to a ghat by the Ganga. Four or five of us (including Kali babu) had to share a room. The walls of that room were covered with pictures of Hindu gods and goddesses. At night, after the lights had been switched off, and I began to doze after a hard day's work, a sudden flash of light would wake me occasionally. When I opened my eyes, I would see Kali babu stretched on the floor, shining a torch on each of those pictures, one by one, and muttering under his breath.

Kali babu's memory wasn't that strong, so he had great difficulty at times in remembering his lines. Not only that, he would get most irritated if anyone tried speaking to him just before a shot. 'Couldn't you find a worse time to come and jabber?' he would bark. 'Can't you see I am trying to get into the right moot?' In spite of getting into the right 'moot' (mood), on one occasion he stumbled again and again over one particular line. The words were 'I have got some tea leaves tied in a corner of my shawl'. Every time he tried to speak that line, the words became either 'shawl leaves in a corner of my tea', or 'my shawl in tea leaves'. By the time he finally got it right, the light had started to fade and we were about to pack up!

We came into contact with a large number of old and middle-aged amateur actors when shooting *Pather Panchali* and *Aparajito*. No other film afterwards required quite so many old men. Most of them were inhabitants of Boral, the village where *Pather Panchali* was shot. One cannot even use the term 'amateur' for many of them for they had never acted anywhere at all. Despite that, none of them seemed to suffer any discomfort when facing the camera. Each followed my instructions easily and did what was required of them quite spontaneously.

One of those men was used in just one scene in *Aparajito*. I had heard that he could sing, so a few years later I offered him a relatively bigger role in *The Postmaster*. He was supposed to sing at a get-together of old men in the village, accompanied by a harmonium, violin and tabla. The gentleman wrote and composed the song himself and announced, 'I will play the harmonium myself.' When I heard his self-composed song, I realized that he had used the raga Ashavari. 'Dadu,' I said, 'the get-together takes place in the evening, after sunset. Do you think this raga will be suitable?' The man remained perfectly unperturbed. After a struggle that lasted just ten minutes, he recomposed the same song, this time in Puravi. The varied emotions and various gestures with which he finally presented the song in front of the camera placed him—quite easily— on par with professional actors, even if he didn't get very far as a singer. The truth is that if an actor is asked to perform before a camera what he does best, easily and spontaneously, his acting is very likely to rate as first-class. In our country, the reason behind weak or faulty acting is very often related to attempts at forcing an actor to do what does not come to him naturally.

When talking of acting and music, mention must be made of Chhabi Biswas. Everyone knows about his relationship with the former. What I am about to relate will explain why I mention the latter. I got to know Chhabi Biswas while making *Jalsaghar*. More than once, for long periods of time, we had to stay in the house owned by the Chowdhuris in a village called Neemtita in Murshidabad. It was impossible to imagine anyone except Chhabi babu in the role of Vishwambhar Ray. However, when I met him to talk about casting, I discovered that though he was ideal for that role, two things were in doubt. First, he had never ridden a horse. Second, he was wholly indifferent to music.

'Do you know the basic notes? Sa re ga ma?'

'I doubt it.'

'Ragas? Raginis? Classical music?'

'Not in the least.'

It might have been possible to teach him to ride, but any attempt made at teaching him to take an interest in music at his age was bound to fail. Although we tried our best, in the end neither could be achieved. In order to shoot the scene where Vishwambhar goes riding his horse, we had to use a 'double' and dress him in Vishwambhar's clothes. The 'double' was said to be the best stuntman not just in Calcutta, but the whole of Bengal. However, his performance was so wonderful in the last scene where Vishwambhar is thrown off the horse to land on sandy ground that I had to abandon every hope of using stuntmen in the future. One single fall made our Khan sahib, the stuntman, take to his bed and remain there for the next three days.

The problem with music could be dealt with far more

successfully. In one scene, Chhabi Biswas was required to play the esraj while his son sang. He had to run a bow over the strings as well as use his fingers to play in harmony with the song. Tireless practice and sheer perseverance made him come through this difficult test with flying colours.

In another scene, Vishwambhar Ray was shown sitting alone on his veranda on a moonlit night. From his neighbour Mahim Haldar's house, strains of music (a khayal) were wafting across. Vishwambhar was listening to it, quite engrossed, his mood melancholy. Clutched in his left hand was his walking stick, his right hand placed over its handle. When the scene was shot, no music was used. All I said to Chhabi babu was, 'As you listen to the music, raise the index finger of your right hand—whenever you want—and strike the stick gently, just once. That is all I want.' When our work on making this film reached its last phase, and we began adding sound to it, the relevant khayal was added to that silent shot with Vishwambhar. It was played in such a way that when Chhabi babu raised his finger and struck a note, it was perfectly in keeping with the rhythm of the song. As a result, no one who understands music can doubt that Vishwambhar was a true connoisseur.

One day, the same Chhabi babu became most concerned about music. As I have said before, during the shooting of *Jalsaghar*, he and I stayed in the same house in Neemtita. We were given rooms at opposite ends of a long and wide veranda. (It was said that the dramatist, Kshirodprasad, had once stayed in my room and written *Ali Baba*.) Our shooting took place in the morning and in the evening. Every day, when dusk fell, Chhabi babu retired to his room and remained there.

That particular evening, we were preparing for the next day's shooting, which would show festivities in the Ray household. A band would play, for which purpose a band had been hired from Murshidabad. It was around half past eight in the evening. I was sitting by a lamp and going through the pages of the script. On the ground floor, facing our veranda, the band was rehearsing and I was occasionally peering out of my window to instruct them to play different tunes. Suddenly, from the opposite end, someone roared, 'Mr Ray!' It was Chhabi babu's voice. I sprang to my feet and came out of the room quickly. Chhabi babu was standing at the edge of the veranda, clasping its railing, looking down and shaking his head impatiently. He saw me in the semi-darkness and pointed at the band. 'What on earth is going on?' he asked most contemptuously.

'It's for tomorrow's shooting, you see. That band will play at the celebration in Vishwambhar's house. So they are rehearsing.'

Chhabi babu roared again. 'Do you call this a band? Neither do they have any rhythm, nor spirit . . . ha!'

I felt a little embarrassed. 'Well sir, in a village, how can you hope to find anything better?' I asked.

Chhabi babu refused to listen. 'No good! This is no good!' he declared, then suddenly turned to me. 'Why don't *you* conduct?'

I had to admit that conducting a band was something I wasn't used to doing. At this, he decided to take matters into his own hands. Within seconds, I found him leaning over the railing most dangerously and, with both his arms raised high, conducting the band himself.

Soon, all that could be heard was his voice, drowning the sound of the band, the jackals and the crickets: 'One two three . . . one two three . . .!'

18

A Quarter of a Century

I have been asked—by a number of people, on many occasions—what new aspects of the art of cinema I have discovered in the last twenty-five years since I made *Pather Panchali*, and how that knowledge has been reflected in my subsequent films. Perhaps the question has come with an added implication: since no other film of mine has received the same accolade, acclaim and awards as *Pather Panchali*, have I really improved or developed as a film-maker in the last twenty-five years?

A brief answer to that question would be: Yes, of course I have, and many of my later films bear evidence of that. I am aware that many people will disagree with my response. The chief asset of *Pather Panchali* was its simplicity. Added to that were deep emotions, poetry, realism and humanitarian qualities—each of which was present in Bibhuti Bhushan's novel. A combination of these qualities has made *Pather Panchali* acquire such a special place in the heart of the audience that the film cannot be removed from there.

As a matter of fact, if a film's greatness could be judged only by its emotional appeal, most certainly *Pather Panchali* would have been my best film in these twenty-five years. But

---

'Shatabdeer Shiki Bhaag', *Anandalok*, Puja Issue, 1980.

no film can be judged just by this single yardstick. Looking at it purely from the point of view of its language, I know *Pather Panchali* suffers from weaknesses in many places only because at the time I did not have enough experience. Fortunately, most of these weak portions occur in the beginning of the film. The order in which the scenes were shot followed, more or less faithfully, the sequence of events in the story, i.e. the scenes described in the beginning of the novel were shot before the ones that came later. There was a long gap between these two phases of shooting. When people hear that it took as much as two-and-a-half years to complete the film, many make sympathetic noises, but we know that the time spent in waiting for fresh funds to resume shooting was really a time to learn more and hone our skills. We assessed and analysed the work we had done, became aware of mistakes made and tried to ensure that all our future work was more efficiently handled.

Although the main aim was to express everything simply, there was one thing that I tried to achieve consciously, even twenty-five years ago. It was to use as little dialogue as possible during the most memorable moments in the film. Needless to say, all those moments came from the original novel. Bibhuti Bhushan made those come to life through a most poetic use of his language. As a film-maker, I had to turn to the language of cinema, not literature. That is why when Apu and Durga see a train for the first time, it cuts across not just an ordinary field—but a field filled with kaash (pampas grass); that is why when Durga sees Indir's inert body and steps back, her foot knocks over the very familiar bronze pot we have all seen before in Indir's hand, and it acquires a life of its own, rolls down a slope and falls into a pool; that is why Apu does not pick up the bead necklace his sister had stolen and throw it away into a bamboo grove (as he does in the novel); he throws it into a pond. The scum on its surface opens up for a moment, then closes over, as if to hide the only unpleasant episode in Durga's life.

***

The same thing can be said about the first four or five films I made—each of them told a simple story in a simple way. The language used in those films might have made an impression, but structurally they did not vary a great deal. From that point of view, the first exception was *Kanchanjungha*, which was based on my own story. It was not just the story that was my own—*Kanchanjungha* was the first film for which I wrote all the dialogue myself. I remember that when I was making *Pather Panchali*, I found it very difficult to alter, even marginally, the dialogue written by Bibhuti Bhushan in his novel. On one occasion, Kanu babu (who played Apu's father) ruined eight shots, one after another, by saying 'luchi-mohanbagan' instead of 'luchi-mohanbhog'.* If such a thing happened today, after the second failed attempt, I would not hesitate to change the words to 'luchi-sandesh' or 'luchi-halwa'. It took me a long time to find the courage to stop being faithful to the original text and write my own words, better suited to cinema.

I watched *Kanchanjungha* with the general audience and realized that the film would not do well commercially because the audience was not used to seeing a whole family as the central character in a film. Yet I really enjoyed introducing the eight characters in the Choudhuri household and building up a network of their relationships, together with a few others, and then presenting and solving the problems of each individual, over a period of one-and-a-half hours. The structure of

---

*Mohan Bagan is the name of a football team; mohanbhog is a sweet.

Kanchanjungha was essentially a cinematic structure, which is something that cannot be said about any of my earlier films.

Among the films that I made in the first ten or twelve years, I think it is *Charulata* (made three years and two films after *Kanchanjungha*) that bears most distinctly the mark of all the experience that I had gained in that time. This can be seen in various aspects of the film, and at various levels—not just in my own work but also that of others who have been a part of my unit from the start.

The slightly sad note on which the film begins vanishes quickly upon the arrival of Manda and Amal. Then the story proceeds in a light-hearted manner, which is followed by suggestions of mixed emotions and varied moods. It reaches its climax in one particular scene. That was the first time I showed such a variety of emotions, hence it is necessary to describe the scene in some detail.

Amal has just finished singing the song *Aami chini go chini* in his Bouthan's presence. Charu is quite pleased with Amal at this moment as she knows that he is not at all keen to get married. She takes his old slippers to her room; she wants to give him a pair of new ones instead, embroidered by her own hands, which she had originally made for her husband. At that very moment, Amal receives word that the *Sararooha* magazine has agreed to publish one of his articles. He goes first to Manda to give her this news as he has promised to buy her kulfi if his article gets published. Charu has only just brought out the new pair of slippers, when she can hear Amal's rapturous announcement: 'Manda Bouthan! *Sararooha* is going to print my article!' For Charu, this is as bad as being struck by lightning. She knows that Amal is about to come to her with the same news, so she stops him by putting the bolt on her door. She remains quite unmoved when he knocks on it.

Outside, Amal and Manda exchange glances and both can immediately grasp the situation. Someone knocks on Charu's door again—but this time it is Bhupati, not Amal. An agitated and confused Charu wipes her eyes and opens the door. She had to close the door because she had seen a cockroach in her room, she says. Innocently, Bhupati believes her, shuts the door himself and leaves a little later, having shown Charu his freshly printed journal and asked her to smell it.

Now Amal arrives with the kulfi. He knows Charu is cross, so he goes and offers it first to Charu, but she refuses to have any. Manda, still standing outside on the veranda, does not wish to make matters worse; so she does not want to eat any kulfi, either ('My teeth hurt,' she declares). It is eventually lapped up by a cat.

No other film of mine—made either before or after *Charulata*—shows four characters thrown into an array of so many conflicting moods in a single sequence running five to seven minutes.

Since the language of a film can make use of visual images, sound, spoken words as well as music, and since cinema is always confined to a specified time limit, the main aim of a director must be to see how briefly, succinctly and appealingly he can express his meaning. It has to be borne in mind at all times that simply uttering a few words about something important is not necessarily going to work. In the story, *Nastaneer*, the final words spoken by Charu are 'Na, *thaak* (no, let it be)' in response to Bhupati's offer to take her to Mysore with him. In that single word 'thaak', there is an obvious suggestion that the gulf between husband and wife is still as wide as ever. However, just that one word, used at the end of the film, would not have made a powerful ending. Only when I was sure of this did I decide, after much deliberation, to use a freeze-shot of the two hands of husband and wife coming close, but not actually meeting.

There is an example in *Aranyer Din Ratri*, which I made ten years ago, of how thoughts and feelings may be conveyed by implication rather than words. From the point of view of film language, I think this film is one of my best, although it did not receive much appreciation in this country.

Somewhere in the middle of the film, by which time we have come to know every character, at least superficially, comes the scene where they play the memory game. Each character retains his or her individuality; yet this scene shows the relationships that have sprung up between them almost without their knowing, and hints at the direction in which each will take them. Nothing is said explicitly, not for a moment does the game stop, but in the end, the game becomes of secondary interest. What rises above it is the suggestiveness in the behaviour of every character.

This particular scene, in which all the characters are exposed through a game, is one of my own favourite scenes. As its creator, I can say—most emphatically—that behind its apparently light-hearted mood lay a lot of careful thought and calculation. Only if the planning and calculation that go into a scene can be hidden from the audience, can the language of a film claim to be successful. Such success cannot be achieved without enough experience and practice.

After having worked for twenty-five years as a film-maker, I can say at least this much with confidence: if I read a good story, or think of one, I can now turn it into something suitable for cinema and present it in a cohesive form. Realistic films, fantasies, films for grown-ups, films for children, comedies, tragedies, historical films and contemporary films—in the last twenty-five years, I have had the chance to try my hand at all of these. Like every other art form, there is no end to learning about the art of cinema. Every time a new kind of story comes along, there will be the need to find a new structure and new language to make a film from it. If an appropriate language isn't readily available, such a language will have to be invented on the basis of one's previous experience.

It is possible to do all these things, but one cannot remain impervious to an existing situation. Sometimes, circumstances can force even an experienced director to follow a set pattern, trite though it might be.

In the mid-1960s, a time came when I began to think that there was no reason why an established and creative director could not find enough work; there was no obstacle in the way of experimenting with new subjects and new styles. But over the last five years I have started to feel—with growing conviction—that such a situation cannot last indefinitely.

In the past few years, the cost of film-making has seen a terrible rise. Added to that has been an absence of reliable equipment; the wretched condition of our studios, laboratories and cinemas; the influence of Hindi films on our audience that has led to a distortion in their taste; and the havoc created by prolonged power cuts. As a result, cinema in Bengal is in such a state today that I do wonder how long I shall be able to apply all that I have learnt in the last twenty-five years.

Filmography

1973   *Ashani Sanket* (Distant Thunder)
1974   *Sonar Kella* (The Golden Fortress)
1975   *Jana Aranya* (The Middleman)
1977   *Shatranj Ke Khilari* (The Chess Players)
1978   *Joi Baba Felunath* (The Elephant God)
1980   *Hirak Rajar Deshe* (The Kingdom of Diamonds)
1984   *Ghare Baire* (Home and the World)
1989   *Ganashatru* (An Enemy of the People)
1990   *Shakha Proshakha* (Branches of a Tree)
1991   *Agantuk* (The Stranger)

SHORT FILMS

1964   *Two* (a.k.a. The Parable of Two)
1980   *Pikoo* (a.k.a. Pikoo's Day)
1981   *Sadgati* (Deliverance)

DOCUMENTARIES

1961   *Rabindranath*
1971   *Sikkim*
1972   *The Inner Eye*
1976   *Bala*
1987   *Sukumar Ray*

Index